I0494808

Fix That Business

John H. Wiig

Copyright © 2012 John H. Wiig

All rights reserved.

ISBN-10: 147514718X
ISBN-13: 978-1475147186

LCCN

DEDICATION

To my parents, Roy and Elaine, who inspired me to think and ask good questions. To my wife Nancy and my three sons, Thomas, Jack and Matt for their invaluable love and support.

CONTENTS

ACKNOWLEDGMENTS

I would like to thank the many fantastic men and women who I have had the pleasure of working with and learning from over the years. I would like to add a special thanks to Ron Buckley for inspiring me to write a book and for providing valuable feedback on my first draft and Eric Peterson for his input on the Bluefish Tournament. I would like to thank Scott Blumenfeld, Bill Gutelius Jr. and Elaine Wiig for the hours they took to thoroughly read the book and provide detailed feedback. Finally I would like to thank the CreateSpace staff and my editor, Michael for his thorough, comprehensive copyediting.

Part I

Background

1

A BRIEF HISTORY

When asked if a glass of water appears half full or half empty, my response has become: there is an opportunity to use a smaller glass. My background is engineering and finance, and my over twenty-five-year career has spanned a variety of manufacturing operations and financial services businesses, including a brokerage firm. I've been involved with countless companies around the globe, offering help and advice on how to operate businesses more efficiently. A number of factors create obstacles when driving changes in businesses, but if you really want to drive meaningful change, this book provides a structured approach and a number of improvement ideas.

Change in a business only happens when it is demanded from the top, or from a leader who has the influence to get the endorsement of senior leadership. One other important attribute of the leader is the ability to navigate a political environment quickly, neutralizing those that resist change. This book contains examples of leaders who accepted jobs in businesses only to find out that they had just joined the leadership team of a company slated for closing or sale because it wasn't generating adequate profit. These leaders were very successful in rallying the support necessary from those above them and knowing how and where to make the right changes in those below them.

A significant factor in how well a business is run can be the competitiveness of its marketplace. The more mature the market, the more competitive it is. The only way to grow a company's market share in a mature market is to take it away from other businesses. Some businesses, however, operate in a space where there is little or no competition, or where the market is continuing to grow and there is no pressure to focus on how efficiently the business runs. Return on investment and profits are both great, and the business continues to grow despite its inefficiencies. But for nearly every business, the day comes when growth slows, profits disappear, and help is needed.

Movement to Lower-Cost Labor Markets

Beginning in the 1970s, when 20 percent of US jobs were in manufacturing, competitive forces caused businesses to consider moving their operations to lower-cost environments.

As any business operates and retains employees over time, one of two things happens. Either the company develops an overpaid workforce relative to the competition, or the company manages to keep wages down, often sacrificing many of their more skilled workers, who leave to seek higher-paying opportunities.

I was very fortunate to begin my career working on a factory floor as a production engineer in Stamford, Connecticut, at a manufacturer that had been there for over fifty years. While the business was profitable, an aged workforce and a factory organized by departments created an expensive and inefficient manufacturing process, making it a great place to learn about improving processes. We knew one of our biggest competitors was operating out of a much newer factory in Salt Lake City, paying labor rates significantly lower than ours. The 1980s brought a period of change, where many companies moved to the lower-cost labor markets of the South.

As an example, I recall the American Thread company in Willimantic, Connecticut. It opened its doors in the 1820s, and it caused the city to earn the nickname, the "Thread City." A landmark bridge in the middle of town has frogs sitting atop large spools of thread. It is all that is left of an industry that employed generations of local families. In the 1980s, that 160-year-old institution closed its doors and moved south to North Carolina, seeking a lower-cost labor market.

My employer in Stamford, with its less-competitive wage structure, found itself in the position of being a small medical-device manufacturer inside a large defense contractor. When the decision was made to divest the medical-device business, the buyer that stepped up was the competitor in Salt Lake City. This factory followed many others and left Stamford in the late 1980s. Today, only a few small manufacturing businesses remain in the city; many have disappeared. Driving through Stamford on I-95, motorists pass buildings that display the names of prominent international banks and other financial services institutions. As in many towns across Connecticut and the United States, Stamford's revenues are no longer derived from a manufacturing base but from a service market.

Just as US businesses were moving to lower-cost domestic labor markets, foreign auto manufacturers came in, looking to build foreign cars on US soil. As they talked to the different states about building an auto manufacturing plant and bringing jobs, each state tried to attract these manufacturers with tax exemptions and training-allowance incentives. These manufacturers played the states against each other to find the best possible deal. Some even recognized the tax benefits of manufacturing in Puerto Rico and set up several manufacturing facilities there. In the 1960s, the first Maquiladora opened its doors in Mexico. Taking advantage of low labor rates in cities just across the Rio Grande, parts were consigned across the United States border in Mexico and returned as assembled goods. The significantly lower labor costs in Mexico made this a logical move. These quests to find lower-cost labor markets continued, and factories opened in India, China, and other low-cost markets in the 1990s.

So this paints the scene of a contracting manufacturing environment. Just after World War II, nearly one in three American jobs were in manufacturing. Today that number is less than one in ten. Two factors that played heavily in this decline are the migration of jobs to a lower labor cost environment and automation.

But that same cost competitiveness has spread to our service markets. In the late 1990s, it became common to call a customer service number and find yourself speaking to someone with a foreign accent over a poorly connected phone line. Over time, the connections improved, and the accents seemed to disappear. Articles flooded papers and magazines describing how some large US companies had shifted their call centers to Asia, and the local Asian companies that provided the service had started giving speech lessons and giving assumed names to their employees to make them sound like people from the Midwestern United States.

While in Bangalore, India, in the late 1990s, I toured a very large modern office tower. What really struck me was not how modern the building was, but how, on one half of the floor, there was a massive room filled with ten-foot-square cubes, and in each corner of the cubes were four work stations with four programmers, programming away. The name on the door was that of a very prominent US conglomerate. Right across the hall was an identical setup. And the name on *that* door was a very prominent US computer and software-services firm. In both cases, the corporations' Indian employees were working for a wage that was probably 20 percent of what people in the United States earned, in office space that cost probably 20 percent of what office space cost in the United States, and the employees' workspace consisted of only 25 percent of the square footage used by their counterparts in the United States.

These are two examples that emphasize the overall trend; labor will find its way to the lowest cost market, and not until the wage rate rises in that lower-cost market to become close to the higher cost market will the job flow out of the higher-cost market cease.

Managing Your Business

The best way to manage these issues is to make your business as efficient as possible. The intent of this book is to provide a simple approach to improve the processes in your business, reduce operating costs, and—most importantly—manage the cultural resistance to change. The book begins by discussing the importance of strategic planning, and how, if it is conducted and deployed properly, it gets everyone in the business working on the same objectives. Businesses lose significant efficiency when all of their functions and departments are not aligned toward pursuing the same vision. The book next discusses the tools for change, identifying methods of improving top-line, performance, and then turns to addressing bottom-line performance. It touches on managing people through change, provides guidance on a few other key points to consider, and then finishes with some concluding remarks.

I limited the length of this book. Given the hectic world in which we live, it made more sense to be concise in sharing my stories, rather than filling the book with content that may not be as valuable. I also intentionally populated the book with examples from financial services as well as manufacturing.

The intent is to explain both types of examples in a very simple and straightforward way so that you can make your own assessment as to whether any of these tactics or strategies can be translated into your industry, regardless of the industry example source. So I encourage all of you to read each section, since you may find an unanticipated benefit.

Part II

Strategic Planning

2

STRATEGIC PLANNING

Over the past twenty-five years, I've worked with many businesses, and I've always tried to get a sense of their level of strategic planning. I put businesses into one of three buckets:

1. Those that use strategic planning where the entire business tactically executes the plan
2. Those that attempt strategic planning, but fail to follow through on tactical execution
3. Those that do not conduct strategic planning.

Let me begin with how I approach strategic planning. The process can be led by someone internally, or an external consultant can be brought in to facilitate the process. Typically the person leading the process will begin by sitting with the CEO and determining who should be interviewed to gather an understanding of how the business is positioned in its current markets. Often this list of people will include the

CEO's direct reports and several leaders one or two levels below the leadership team. I strongly recommend that anyone who is interviewed is cleared with the CEO first. Within a few weeks of the interviews, I pull all the people interviewed together for an offsite meeting to formulate a Strategic Plan. It's best to keep the number of participants below twenty, and I absolutely avoid having more than thirty people involved. Larger groups become more difficult to facilitate.

The feedback from all the interviews is reviewed and organized to create an outline of the Strategic Plan to be reviewed with the CEO. After the review with the CEO, an offsite meeting with all the people interviewed, the facilitator, and the CEO will take place for two days to produce the business-strategy document. The last part of the process involves the facilitator attending the CEO's staff meeting to make sure all functions are executing on the strategic initiatives that were defined in the offsite meeting.

To begin the process, the CEO identifies who will facilitate the Strategic Planning process. The facilitator meets with the CEO and identifies who should be interviewed. The interviews should all take place within a one-week period, and the meetings with each person should run just under an hour.

SWOT and the Porter Model

I endorse the classic strategic planning approach of understanding a business's Strengths, Weaknesses,

Opportunities, and Threats, which is referred to as the SWOT method.

The "Porter Model" view, also known as the Porter "Five Forces" view of the business, is based on Michael Porter's famous 1979 *Harvard Business Review* article that defined the five forces that impact any business:

1. The bargaining power of customers
2. The bargaining power of suppliers
3. The threat of new entrants
4. The threat of substitutes
5. The rivalry among competitors.

If someone in the company has created the Porter Model for the business, whoever facilitates this session can benefit from reviewing it prior to the interviews. It is a great tool for understanding where a business sits relative to all five forces, and can help the facilitator ask better questions.

As I mentioned earlier, a business with few if any competitors, few if any new entrants, and no current substitutes faces much different competitive forces than those of a business in a mature market. If the business does not have a Porter Model built, it may be worth pulling a few key players together and quickly assembling one before starting the interview process. It is important to emphasize that the process around Strategic Planning is not complicated.

One other important step to take in preparation is to get a copy of the business's financial statements. Review the profitability by product line and by products, if that level of detail is available. Review how costs have been allocated by the product and perform a quick check to see if they are consistently distributed by sales volume. This review should be conducted before the individual interviews, as it could influence which questions are asked.

The Five Whys

For a successful strategic planning session, you want a strong facilitator who engages the entire team and pushes hard at the appropriate time by "asking *why* five times." When encountering an industry-accepted norm, we need to question *why* it is an accepted norm. In some cases, it may be based on issues that are no longer relevant today. When the first *why* question is asked about the industry norm, an answer is provided, leading to another question asking *why* to that answer. The intent is not to frustrate the audience, but to determine *why* the norm in question is an industry-accepted norm, and whether it should be accepted today. The right facilitator knows how and when to ask these questions, tactfully yet forcefully, to get the audience to think carefully about the issue. Known as the "Five Whys" in the world of process improvement, this line of questioning is a great approach to addressing industry norms that should not exist.

An example of the *five whys* involves a newly hired Vice President of Manufacturing, who was touring the production floor when he came upon a workbench covered in neatly-organized, small plastic sensors used in medical procedures.

When he questioned the operator as to why they were there, he was told they were recently put together with epoxy, and they had to sit overnight to cure. What the vice president saw was money unnecessarily tied up in inventory, so he asked why we can't use an epoxy that dried faster. The operator responded by saying he did not know. The supervisor who heard the conversation stepped in and told the vice president that the design engineer would have to be asked. The engineer was then promptly called out to the production floor. When the vice president asked the engineer about an epoxy that cures faster, he said that the two-part epoxy was the only adhesive that had been approved for this product. "Why can't you find an epoxy that dries faster?" the vice president asked. The engineer responded that he knew of an epoxy that cured under ultraviolet light, but it would have to be tested and approved. "Why don't we start working on that?" the vice president asked. Needless to say in less than a month, the epoxy was changed, and the parts no longer sat overnight.

The Interview Questions

Once a Porter Model is in place, here are some great questions to ask each person who is interviewed. This list is in no particular order, and can be changed to exclude or add some questions based upon the client or the industry. I might consider adding a question or two if something significant comes up in an interview.

1. Does your business have a vision statement that is written or verbally communicated?
2. Who do you see aligned to that vision—every function, some functions, management?
3. What is your businesses strategy?
4. How do your customers perceive your business?
5. What do your customers value the most?
6. What do your customers value most, and will it be the same in three years?
7. What industry trends do you see having the greatest effect on the business?
8. What do you see as important to this business in three years—where should it be?
9. What are your business' top three Strengths?
10. What are your top three Weaknesses?
11. What are your top three Opportunities?
12. What do you see as the top three Threats to the business?
13. How would you describe the Information Technology (IT) systems and core business processes?
14. If you could upgrade or improve three systems and/or processes, which three would you select?
15. How do you view the talent level of the people?
16. Are there areas where the business is underperforming?
17. Are there any structural issues with the business?
18. How would you describe the business' culture?
19. What areas of leadership could be improved?
20. What other important issues do you see?

I also like to ask people I interview if there are other people I should consider interviewing that they feel have good strategic insight into the business. If one person's name is mentioned several times in the interviews, but is not on my list of people to interview, I will go back to the CEO to ask if that person should be included. Keep in mind that this process ultimately involves pulling the entire group together to establish the go-forward strategy. In that meeting, sometimes a random idea may be raised that could trigger someone else to consider a different perspective. That new perspective could influence the direction the business strategy takes. Getting the right people involved in this process is critical to finding the optimal strategy for the business.

After the interviews are complete, all the feedback is compiled to get an effective view of the business' Strengths, Weaknesses, Opportunities, and Threats. From this, there may be a series of follow-up questions for several of the interview candidates, which are typically done on the phone. Next, I meet with the CEO to present the high-level observations and to review the format and agenda for the upcoming offsite meeting. From this meeting, the two-day offsite meeting is set up.

All those interviewed are required to attend. Calendars have to be cleared, and all cell phones are to be turned off. Everyone has to be there for the entire meeting. If you must schedule it on a weekend in order to get everyone there, then select a weekend. Collectively, the group will work through the feedback, and from the ensuing discussion, they will assemble the Strategic Plan.

When the two days are over, a Strategic Plan has been created that may require a minor tweak or two.

Executing the Plan

Now is a good time to reemphasize a point I made earlier. Strategic planning can be done effectively with coordinated tactical execution, or effectively with poor tactical execution, or not at all. In that second case where, there is poor tactical execution that situation can happen because the right people in the business were not engaged in the strategic planning process. By having an offsite that engages the entire leadership team, everyone gets a say in the Strategic Plan. Many businesses will leave it to a small group to conduct strategic planning, and thereby lose engaging the entire business.

A telltale sign that no collaboration existed in defining the Strategic Plan happens when the CEO issues his goals for the year and several of his direct reports issue very different goals. To be competitive, you need to be like a good sports team, where everyone reads from the same playbook and understands the need to work together and grow the business.

When you think about it, no one ever stays the same; one either gets better or gets worse. Those words are paraphrased from a quote that a former business leader had framed and placed on the wall in the office area for everyone to see. In my experience, those words ring true. Make sure your team follows the same playbook and is made up of people looking to get better.

In formulating the Strategic Plan, businesses should be targeting three to five major objectives during the course of the year. For each objective, there are tactical actions that must be addressed. When any operating change is introduced to a business, it will often be met with skepticism. Some leaders may label this as the "flavor of the day," assuming that this new approach will soon disappear once the next "flavor" comes along. Any executive who understands the tremendous synergy that is achieved by aligning the business to a common set of goals knows the value of setting up a ninety-day, one-year, and three-year Strategic Plan. Failing to put the appropriate emphasis on long-term strategy can weaken a business in today's competitive marketplace. To make these changes stick, the facilitator needs to regularly attend the CEO's staff meeting. That meeting has to consistently review activity against the strategic objectives, and determine whether attempts to meet those objectives are on-track.

At this point, it might be worth our while here to discuss leadership styles. In general terms, we can describe two types of leaders, those who are market facing and customer/sales oriented and those who are operations focused and tend to concentrate on how the business operates, including the employees and the processes.

The Market-Focused Leader

Let's call the first one a market-focused leader, and the second an operations-focused-leader. A great example of these two contrasting leadership approaches can be seen in General Electric. In the 1980s and 1990s, GE leadership was focused on getting its businesses to be number one or number two in their marketplace. This strategy led to a significant restructuring of the business.

Consider the position of power that a market-leading business has. It can often adjust prices in the marketplace, and most others will follow. That is a powerful position to be in. These market leaders have a competitive advantage that takes some of the complexity out of running their business.

I ran into a similar situation at Hubbell, when one business general manager commented to another (who was busy restructuring his business) that when his business started to fall short of meeting its numbers, he just raised his prices. This is the power of being a market leader, and these businesses are typically run by a market-focused leader. Businesses that do not have that market-leadership position can often be niche players that are subject to what the market will bear in price.

The Operations-Focused Leader

Now consider the simple equation below:

Profit=Price-Cost

If price is set in the marketplace, the only lever to improve profitability is through cost cutting. These businesses need a strong operating leader among the senior ranks. A common practice at GE in the 1980s and 1990s was a formal process around reviewing talent in the business. Understanding the strengths and development needs of the people in the business, and how those needs are addressed, is critical. A true operating leader knows the importance of putting the right people in the right jobs where they can best contribute to improving her company. The GE approach in the 1980s and 1990s put strong focus on reviewing talent in the business through a robust performance-review process that included top leadership involvement. Beyond the goal of managing and developing the people in the business was that of getting the business leaders to focus on driving top- and bottom-line performance improvements.

By giving each business leader an increased revenue and profit target, the business leaders were forced to pursue cost-reduction strategies. Since every business leader was not an operating manager, this forced market-focused business leaders to look internally for cost reductions when the market challenges were preventing them from reaching their top-line numbers. Evidence of this approach can be seen in GE's not adopting Lean (a practice of eliminating wasteful activities in any business process) as a global initiative until 2004, long after many other businesses, which had embarked on Lean in the 1970s and 1980s.

In the mid-1990s, when I was involved in a medical-device manufacturer's turnaround, we often played a short, thirty-minute video cassette made in 1983 by our number-one competitor, demonstrating the throughput gains of reduced batch sizes—a fundamental aspect of Lean. We explained to the people in the business that as we were embarking on a conversion to Lean manufacturing, our major competitor was already twelve years ahead of us. While we successfully rolled Lean out in less than a year across the entire factory, we ultimately became but one of several small pockets of GE businesses using Lean at that time.

Thus, the strategy introduced at GE in the 1980s was to replicate the classic turnaround strategy of exiting the less-competitive businesses, then taking the remaining market-leading businesses and forcing them to improve further by hitting increased profitability every year. If the top-line number became unattainable, cost-reduction opportunities helped companies to achieve the goal.

After ten or fifteen years of being a top-performing business and having trimmed unnecessary costs to achieve those increasing net income numbers, maintaining double-digit revenue and profit growth-rate percentages becomes very difficult. The business strategy needs to identify a way of expanding the target market to make the business a smaller percentage of the overall market, thus creating a larger customer base. At this point, the logical leader for a business is one who can drive growth in the marketplace. Interestingly, in 2001, GE leadership shifted to a growth leader who is very focused on delivering advanced technological solutions to customers, and with that approach, driving growth. Now that an operating leader and a market leader have been defined, you can see how their leadership styles can influence the strategies a business targets.

Return to Strategic Planning

Let's get back to strategic planning. When introducing any type of change in a business, it is much easier if you have a strong operating leader who is more focused internally on the business. One who understands that to be successful at driving process changes, such as introducing strategic planning; the other leaders in the business have to change their behavior. Most people do not readily accept change. Skilled operating leaders know that it takes continued emphasis over a long period of time to drive a behavioral change. GE made one- and three-year strategic planning a core activity in every business. Routine presentations to the CEO and the leadership team were required. For smaller businesses, the leader or facilitator driving the Strategic Plan has to sit in on CEO staff meetings and demand weekly feedback from the key players to verify that the targeted milestones are being achieved.

Now that I have introduced strategic planning, it is important to understand the benefits associated with it. I cannot count the number of organizations I've dealt with in which every member of the leadership team was off pursuing his or her own individual agenda. The common thread in all these businesses was that they either did not have strategic planning, or they had strategic planning, but were not enforcing the execution of the plan. Referring back to the three buckets I put businesses in, these are the businesses that fall in buckets two and three.

Manufacturing Business Example

To provide an example of the benefits of a team-generated Strategic Plan, imagine a business that makes two products, A and B. Product A represents 85 percent of what the business creates, and B represents 15 percent. In this company, the engineering manager has chosen to cost reduce product B to get it down close to the cost of product A, with the intent of replacing product A with an improved product B. But no analysis was done on what could be done to reduce the cost of product A. Perhaps the same expenditure of time and money could reduce the cost of product A by 25 percent? Who, then, would be in favor of the expenditure on Product B? This is a classic case of the Opportunity in a Strengths, Weaknesses, Opportunities, and Threats (SWOT) analysis.

In the interview process, when strategic opportunities are identified, the Engineering Manager would raise the opportunity on cost reducing product B, but that idea would likely be discussed in interviews with other leaders. The decision not to focus on product A would be raised in the two-day offsite, and the appropriate approach would be defined. Since the offsite would include all the key leaders, it would provide a great opportunity for each side to present—with the data to back their case—the merits of cost reducing product A versus cost reducing product B. This is the ideal situation to address this type of issue, and when the final decision is made, everyone has to agree to move forward in support of that decision. The decision could be to do a part of both cost-reduction exercises, or just one, or it could be to conduct a refined study in order to make a decision in thirty to sixty days. This forum minimizes the resources focused on side projects that do not align with the business's Strategic Plan. I have to reemphasize that without these issues being raised and addressed, critical resources could be wasted working on cost-reduction projects that may never be implemented. Businesses have limited resources, and those resources need to be focused to synergistically work towards the same goal.

A Lending Business Example

Another example of the benefits of applying strategic planning involves a lending business that saw a business reorganization shift the decision-making authority on all potential investments to a different final approver. The new approver opposed this type of lending to customers with riskier business models, perceiving the business as too weak to compete in that space. Through a strategic planning process, this product line would become a discussion topic and would be reviewed so that a decision on whether the product should remain active could be made by the CEO with the input of everyone in the room.

A Service Organization Example

A final example involves a service organization within company XYZ that observed company ABC offering to service company XYZ's products. A junior service manager saw competitor ABC's actions as a threat to the continued growth of the service business. While the junior service manager was convinced it was a valid threat, the head of service was convinced that the competitor would not be successful and was opposed to the idea of servicing the competitor's equipment. The junior service manager sold this idea to the finance manager and the marketing manager instead, and they were then able to include this idea as a Threat in the Strengths, Weaknesses, Opportunities, and Threats (SWOT) Analysis. It received senior-level consideration, where it was discussed, and the recommendation to service Company XYZ's products was approved.

These examples help demonstrate the value of strategic planning in a business. It does not matter how small your business is. Take a business with less than $10 million in revenues. There needs to be a plan in place to grow that business. Leveraging the Strengths, Weaknesses, Opportunities, and Threats (SWOT) analysis as part of strategic planning can make that happen and improve nearly any business's competitive position.

When we think about translating the Strategic Plan into tactical actions, there are some great tools and approaches that can be leveraged to achieve an improved performance. The first and most important approach is to create a series of business goals at each level in the business. There are two ways I've seen this accomplished. If a business is working from an established Strategic Plan, the goals all flow directly out of the plan. They begin with the CEO's goals, and trickle down. The second approach I've seen is having goals written at the lowest level in the organization. These goals are then funneled up, and they are used as a source of ideas for the goals the business finally settles upon. This exercise is always best done in advance of the strategic planning session, since it provides ideas for discussion. Often, someone on the front lines in the business may be getting feedback on customer needs, and that feedback may not be getting through to the leadership team as the message gets misinterpreted along the way or maybe never even reaches that level of the organization.

Understanding the Cycle

Finally, every business is confronted with an economic cycle. This plays a role in the business's Strategic Plan. A great business leader needs to anticipate industry changes, and one of them is the economic shift as a country's economy heads into a recession. A great example of what I'm referring to comes from the commercial aircraft finance space. A small lending business, a subsidiary of a large French bank, was lending money, using commercial aircraft as collateral. These loans often had an 80-percent loan-to-value ratio. An example of a loan-to-value ratio is when a lender will lend up to $32 million to a company that wanted the money to buy a $40 million aircraft. The industry was coming from a period when air travel had grown rapidly, and a shortage of many aircraft types had caused some of these aircraft values to rise over time, while all other forms of transportation, like automobiles, devalued with time.

When the recession hit in July 1990, coupled with the war in Kuwait and the recent memories of the Lockerby bombing, people stopped flying. The drop-off in air travel resulted in airline bankruptcies and the parking of many aircraft. With all these parked aircraft, values started dropping. Some planes lost 30 percent, 40 percent, and even 50 percent of their value. This small lending business experienced losses of $70 million on a $350-million portfolio of loans.

Coming out of that experience, the leaders of the business began tracking two metrics that, when combined, allowed them to predict the industry cycle, which closely mirrored the economic cycle. By tracking the change in growth rate of available seats, and the change in growth rate of the demand for seats, they could see the shift in demand and recognize that the economy was about to change. This method allowed for the successful prediction of the downturn of the aviation cycle in late 2007, when nearly everyone else was talking about positive growth into the next decade. This small business has been a consistent performer since, with economic losses that totaled only thirteen basis points over the first twelve years of this century. The business credits its improved performance on its ability to predict the economic cycle along with their improved modeling tools that include the cycle prediction.

Companies that lead the economic cycle by slowing early and recovering sooner often have to have the ability to detect shifts in the economic cycle. A good analyst who understands the industry trends and economic cycles should be a valued contributor to the strategic planning process, regardless of whether the business leads, falls in sync with, or lags behind the economic cycle.

Managing the Backlog

Another critical element is the businesses backlog. First, you must break the process of getting leads into different stages. There may be naturally occurring break points in the process of turning a lead into an order or an investment opportunity—usually at those moments when the probability of that lead becoming an order increases. Use these points to separate your process into stages.

Let's say there are three stages: early, middle, and late. For some companies, you can take all the leads in the early stage and estimate that 20 percent will become an order or a deal. Then look at those that have progressed to the middle stage of the conversion process and estimate that 45 percent of those will become an order or a deal. Finally, take those in the later stage and estimate that 75 percent of those will become an order or a deal. Defining the stages and the percent that actually become an order or a deal will be different for every business, and these percentage that convert should be based on historic data and future estimates, but tracked over time.

Multiplying each stage's conversion rate by the dollar value of orders or deals in that stage and summing that product for all three stages gives you a dollar value you can compare to your monthly volume. This is a great indicator of your order or deal flow. This approach provides much more detail around how your order or deal book is performing and allows you to react sooner than you would with the traditional method of just tracking the dollar value of a backlog. If a business migrates over to Lean and converts orders quickly, regardless of whether it is a manufacturer or financial services business, that business needs a better measure of order or deal flow. Now think back to the section where we discussed the aircraft-lending business that tracked the industry cycle. We can match this backlog, or order-stream metric, against the cycle prediction to determine if any observed volume changes are industry driven or unique to that business.

Please take a moment to review this last sentence; the value of comparing those two metrics cannot be overstated.

Drivers of Profitability

To keep your business growing, determine what drivers influence profitability. These drivers can be many different things. A great example of a driver that will impact profitability comes from the wire and cable business. There were commodities we used like copper and aluminum that were tracked regularly since they could quickly turn profitable sales orders into losses if the pricing became volatile.

Another example of profitability drivers comes from the lending world. A lending business underwrote a loan for a business that manufactured drywall or sheetrock. The underwriting analyst astutely noted that if the price of gypsum, a major component in drywall, rose above 78¢ per pound, they needed to sell their position in the loan. When the analyst was promoted and the loan was transferred to a different analyst, the new analyst never reviewed the file and did not realize the importance of tracking the price of gypsum. Needless to say, the price of gypsum took off, and the business could not pay the loan and defaulted. A postmortem on the deal revealed the recommendation to sell the position in the loan if the price of gypsum rose to 78¢ a pound. Since the business was still very profitable at that point, the loan could have been sold to another lender and the lending business could have avoided the loss. This knowledge allowed the lending business to change the way it tracked all its loans to avoid these costly mistakes in the future.

Drivers to profitability may include product mix, service volumes, pricing programs, and sales incentives. It is up to the CFO to identify and track the performance of each of these drivers and review them with the leadership team on a regular basis. Each driver needs a person's name next to it to show who is accountable to ensure that the identified driver performs at or above the desired level.

Increasing the Business's Competitiveness

Once a Strategic Plan has been defined, the business needs to embark on driving changes and improvements that will increase its competitiveness in the marketplace. Among the options that should be considered are both top-line and bottom-line growth strategies that will now be covered in the next few sections.

Part III

Tools for Change

3

SALES FORCE EFFECTIVENESS

Many businesses provide a significant opportunity to study three specific areas that can drive top-line growth for the company: Sales-Force Effectiveness, Pricing, and Client Retention. These are the topics of the next three chapters.

Sales Force Effectiveness

This section will walk through three examples that led to surprising discoveries for business leaders who conducted a thorough analysis of their business. The questions below touch on three keys to improving a sales force's effectiveness:

1. What is the strategy the salesperson takes with the customer?
2. How are the territories set up, and are they the right size to reach the customer base in the region?

3. Is the sales team properly trained to quickly understand if an initial discussion can grow into a lead that becomes a sale?

Sales Strategy

The head of the sales side of an aircraft-leasing business agreed to tackle a project on improving the conversion rate of potential deals. In that exercise, a key takeaway that resulted had to do with the sales team's approach to the customers. Because it was a lending and leasing business, the sales team called on the CFO or the fleet planner to explore opportunities. The head of sales in this leasing company had come up through the ranks of the sales team, and truly understood what was needed to be successful. In his case, he had developed what he called his "Three F" (3F) Strategy. In preparing to call on the customer, he always reviewed the Franchise, Fleet, and Financials of that customer.

By *Franchise,* he meant how they made money. He'd ask, "What's the business model?" By *Fleet,* he meant, "What aircraft do they currently have, and what will be their needs in the future?" By *Financials,* he meant, "What does their balance sheet look like? Can a purchase and leaseback of an aircraft provide them with the cash they need in the short term? What other aircraft transactions can strengthen the company's position?"

When the sales leader was studying the process, he found that more than half of his sales force was not applying the 3F approach. Since he had discussed this strategy with many members of his sales team, and they were familiar with it, he assumed that they all were following that same approach, but they were not. To resolve that issue, a training session was organized, and after every sales rep was trained, the sales leader observed a lift in volume as the sales reps began using the 3F approach.

Sales Territories

This second example involves understanding the proper sales-force territory size. A sales leader, who had a team of sales reps across the country leasing medical equipment to hospitals and diagnostic centers, had the objective of trying to grow sales. As he studied the entire sales process, he made some surprising observations regarding several territory changes that had been made. Sales reps who'd had their territories reduced had actually seen their volume increase. Not only had their volume increased, but so had the volume of the sales reps who'd taken over the balance of the territory. After some discussion, it was agreed to further increase the number of sales reps to observe the impact.

There was a top-performing sales rep covering Chicago, Wisconsin, and Minnesota. When his territory was first cut, he was left with Chicago and Wisconsin. In the time period following that cut, both the sales rep with the smaller territory of Chicago and Wisconsin did more volume then he had done with all three territories and the new rep for

Minnesota did more volume in Minnesota than was done in the prior year. Based on that improved performance, the sales leader took the next natural step. He cut the sales rep's territory again, giving him just Wisconsin. And now three separate reps were covering Minnesota, Wisconsin, and Chicago, and all three did higher volumes, with the top-performing rep doing a higher volume of business with just Wisconsin than he had when he'd had Chicago, Minnesota, and Wisconsin. And again, the sales reps taking over his former territories of Minnesota and Chicago saw larger levels of growth in those territories than the prior year. The data showed that in all territories where the sales reps' areas were reduced, higher levels of growth appeared than in areas left unchanged. The challenge the business faced was the classic example of not being able to get enough time in front of the potential clients because the territory was too large.

Training Sales Reps

My final example involves properly training your sales reps. The business leader of a large equipment-leasing company wanted to increase his sales. He wondered if there was something different about the sales reps who produced the highest volume, versus those who produced lower volumes. In this case, he used the tools of Six Sigma to identify what unique skill the more-successful sales reps had. For example, was it their number of years as a sales rep? Was it the size of their territory? Was it their number of years with the company? Nearly thirty factors were recorded and studied.

Out of these thirty possible factors, only one was discovered that had a significant effect on sales performance. When that factor was identified, the company's business leader was able to make changes in the training process for the sales reps, driving some very nice top-line growth for the business. The specifics of what he discovered are detailed in the upcoming section on Six Sigma.

Hopefully, these three examples will help you to rethink how you are managing your sales team, and allow you to identify an opportunity to improve how they operate, translating into top-line growth.

4

PRICING

Many businesses believe they have a pricing policy that is consistently applied across the business. Frequently, this is not the case. Recall the earlier story of the general manager who had been speaking with another division manager of a business that was a market leader. That division manager just raised prices, and most of the company's competitors raised their prices too. But at that time, the general manager's business was in a competitive struggle because the boom years before the recession caused significant supply-side capacity to be added. With the downturn, demand dropped, and everyone took any price in order to sell the product to keep market share. It is a tough place to be when the market has complete control over the price.

Pricing is the most powerful lever a business has. Given the choice between a 2-percent reduction in cost, and a 2-percent increase in price, we should all jump at the opportunity to raise price. The top line grows, which should always be a larger value than the total of all costs in the business.

A great example for understanding the effect of the competition's pricing involves a self-service gas station. This gas station was on a main road running through several towns and had nearly twenty gas stations within a five-mile radius. Before the station opened at 6:00 a.m., the attendant would drive five miles in each direction on the road the station was on, just to capture the competition's pricing. Based on the prices gathered, the prices at this self-service station were set to be below the competition. The station's strategy was simply to be the low-cost provider, and they gathered pricing data daily to maintain their position. If you can survive at that pricing level, that is a powerful position to occupy.

Keep in mind, though, that a filling station is in a highly competitive market. Is your business in a highly competitive market? Do you have the ability to study your competition's pricing and set yours at a more favorable level? Obviously, these points play into how you define your business strategy.

Even if a business has a well-defined pricing strategy and does a great job gathering information from the marketplace, there are frequently breakdowns in the pricing process that cause the business to charge less than it should and lose valuable income. Here are a few examples of how the process can break down.

The first example involves a brokerage that had several thousand financial advisors, who were responsible for pricing all trades. But think about the role of the financial advisor. Financial advisors want to keep their clients happy so that the clients continue investing with them. The commission on trades can be a very touchy subject with some clients. When the business reviewed all trade pricing across the business, significant inconsistencies became apparent. Financial advisors were not following a consistent pricing practice. This prompted the business to review the pricing policy, comparing it with some data on the competition. The policy was revised, but not rolled out across the board. Informational sessions and training sessions were conducted, while the changes were piloted in a few test markets. The pilot allowed the business to gather feedback on how the financial advisors and the customers reacted to the changes. A few minor modifications were made based on the pilot, but the revenue increase from introducing these changes was substantial.

There are two important things to notice here. The first issue: When frontline employees who work with customers are given discretion around pricing, management will have very little control over pricing. Even if you have a pricing policy in place, unless you are verifying adherence to the policy, you will not have control. Once a salesperson or a financial advisor executes a transaction with a customer and the pricing was outside the policy, that situation needs to be followed up on immediately. It is the business's choice on how to handle it. If you do not follow up on a transaction priced outside the policy, more transactions outside the policy will continue until the issue is raised.

The second important issue: When rolling out a change of this magnitude, it is important to have a robust process for introducing the new policy. It is prudent to conduct a pilot and have regular conversations with the participants to gather feedback on the changes. There may be necessary adjustments before the changes are rolled out across the business. It is always easier to make changes with a small group. Rolling changes out to the entire business and getting feedback that results in more changes will attack the credibility of the group making the changes and increase the likelihood of errors.

Another example of an issue in the pricing process involves an equipment finance company set up in multiple countries across Europe. It provided loans to companies to purchase such equipment as printing presses, vertical machining centers, or forklifts. When lending a business money, it had to cover the cost of the money, plus put a profit component in the interest rate applied to the loan. To set the interest rate, the business created rate sheets that were sent to every office. Any loan had to be priced using that rate sheet.

In reviewing the pricing process, the analysis involved gathering all the recently priced deals and taking the difference between the rate used on the deal and on the current rate card. When the data was plotted, we instantly knew there was a problem. The data was very inconsistent. For the type of plot that was being used, there should have been a vertical line running up the middle of the graph, with two short tails, one going to the right on the top, and one going to the left on the bottom. Instead, there were about five small vertical lines spread across the page with small tails connecting them. The plots are depicted below.

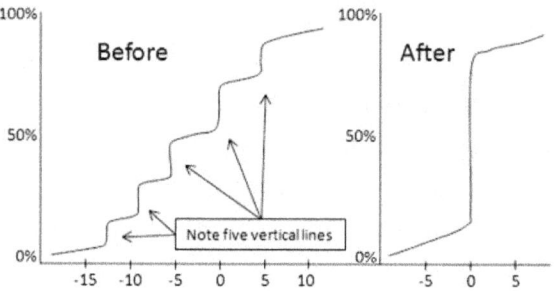

Those of us familiar with this type of graph recognized that there was a problem with the process. We had the analysis team ask every office for a copy of its current rate sheet. In doing so, they discovered that many offices were working with rate sheets that were one, two, or three revisions old. As interest rates had changed, the pricing team had been sending updated rate sheets, but they'd never received confirmation that the new sheets had been received and were being used.

Accordingly, the process was corrected to include a formal distribution where the new rate sheet was issued and the old rate sheet was returned. If the pricing group did not receive the old rate sheet from one of the offices, they followed up. This solved the problem, and interestingly, when the business discovered that the offices had all been working off different rate sheets, they matched the actual rate sheet used for each loan against the prices charged and found that the offices were doing a great job applying the rates from the rate sheets they had. It was important to check this to make sure there were not multiple breakdowns in the process. When they did this match, and plotted the data, it matched the shape in the second plot above, showing good, consistent pricing.

This last pricing example is not about a breakdown in the process, but about an opportunity that the business never knew existed. A consumer finance business in Europe chose to study the United Kingdom market for automobile loans. The team collected data—and not just the pricing data, but demographic data on the neighborhood of the dealerships as well as the size of the dealership, the type of product (loan versus lease), type of cars (luxury, SUV, economy) and many more. After analyzing the data, they discovered two dealerships, nearly identical in size and neighborhood demographics, where one was getting much better pricing. When they investigated the dealerships, the reasoning was simple: the dealership with higher pricing had a finance manager who charged a higher interest rate on the loan or lease. Most customers did not know rates, allowing the finance manager to charge a higher price to increase revenue. This relates to understanding the market and knowing what price it will bear. Any rise in pricing can have a significant effect on the revenue of a business.

I will close with another story that is relevant to the subject of pricing. One business strategy is to be the low-cost supplier of a product. I was involved with a manufacturing business that made a product line of electronic medical devices in the

United States and was losing money, so the business was being offered for sale. A group of savvy leaders in that business saw the opportunity to move the product overseas to a lower-cost labor market to reduce the cost of making that product. When breaking down the cost of a product, direct labor would be about 5 percent to 7 percent of a product's cost and material would be about 60 percent to 70 percent; the rest is *overhead*—the allocated costs of all groups that directly support manufacturing and ancillary materials required to manufacture the product (Quality Assurance, Process Engineering, Purchasing, Scheduling, Materials Planning, and miscellaneous consumables). When you move a product to a lower-cost market, labor is not the source of the big savings. The opportunity lies in the materials and overhead portion of the product. When the product moves to the lower-cost labor market, the subcomponents used to build the product are moved as well. Now that the subcomponents are produced in the local market by local vendors, the subcomponents become much less expensive. As mentioned, material cost in a product is often 60 percent or more. By sourcing subcomponents having a labor and overhead component from the local market, can drop material costs from over 60 percent to below 40 percent, and most of that difference drops to the bottom line. That savings goes right into the medical device moved to the lower-cost labor market. Using the new labor, materials, and overhead for the medical device, and targeting a 20-percent margin, the price of the product can be dropped by as much as 30 percent. In one case, a competitor was forced to match that 30-percent price reduction just to keep market share. It was later discovered that the competitor was actually selling its product below cost, just to keep its market share. This helps explain the disappearance of manufacturing from the United States. But it is important to note that this company manufactured its product using an inefficient "work order" process, and it produced its product in three of the most expensive areas in the world to make a product. It could have been far more competitive if it was a Lean manufacturer in a lower-cost US-based labor market.

The big takeaway here is twofold. First, understand your market and see if there is an opportunity to raise pricing. Second, understand your process for pricing your products and/or services. Frequently, even in the best of companies, the process can break down and create pricing errors that can cost a business millions of dollars.

5

CUSTOMER RETENTION

If you have ever been involved with a startup, you know that one of the most important costs to track is the cost of getting and keeping a customer. Startup companies often stop tracking this cost sometime after they become profitable. Understanding this cost is a valuable measure for nearly every business. In most cases, the cost of retaining a customer is far less than trying to find a new one. But I've seen a few businesses with the attitude that they should not spend time pursuing customers who are considering moving to a competitor.

A great example comes from commercial lending. If a customer has the opportunity to reduce the cost of the money borrowed from a commercial lender, he will often move to a different lender. There was a commercial lender that had accepted the loss of these customers for years, since it was perceived to be an industry norm. The business reviewed its past performance and observed that there were customers who were retained when they wanted to refinance. They studied the customers to understand why they stayed. In most cases, the commercial lender had maintained a good relationship with the customer and was able to get advanced notice of their decision to refinance the loan. The commercial lender worked with their customer-facing teams to change their long-standing acceptance of the industry norm of not seeking refinance opportunities with current customers. This point illustrates what was raised earlier in the strategic planning section. Industries seem to develop "norms" or attitudes that certain things will exist and should be accepted. Once again, asking "why" five times can help eliminate these situations.

In any business, it is worth your time to go through and analyze the patterns and trends appearing in your customer base. Do you see differing levels of customer retention among the company's different sales representatives? Is it regional, or possibly related to the influence of the regional sales manager? There are many questions to ask, and it is worth doing the analysis to understand your customer base.

6

LEAN

The most effective way to take cost out of a business is to introduce Lean. *Lean* is short for *Lean manufacturing.* Lean manufacturing is composed of several techniques that include understanding value-added versus non-value-added activity, Kanban Pull manufacturing, Just-in-Time manufacturing, and vendor-managed inventory. I have applied Lean in a number of settings, both in manufacturing and financial services settings.

Today, Lean is often paired with Six Sigma, but I want to begin by separating the two. Lean is fundamentally the streamlining of all activity in a business. Six Sigma is a tool for using the data in a business to solve problems, including many problems where there is no known answer. This section will begin first by covering Lean and then move into Six Sigma.

Lean involves streamlining processes, with particular emphasis on the core business process. The term *value-*

stream mapping is associated with Lean, because people implementing Lean may choose to create a process map that identifies value-added and non-value-added activity. Any business has a core business process. In a manufacturer of electronic medical devices, a process map would show every step required to order and receive the raw materials and subassemblies, straight through to the shipping of the finished product. Some find it valuable to spend the time it takes to build these maps and then determine where changes can be implemented. Other ways to convert to Lean requiring less work are covered in this chapter. An example of Lean involves a medical-device manufacturer who applied Lean, improving throughput on a medical monitor from over twelve weeks to assemble, test, and ship a medical monitor to less than five days. The inventory and labor savings around these transformations was impressive.

Introducing Lean

In my experience, businesses benefit from Lean in the early stages of their transformation to an improved operating model. After this, Six Sigma should be introduced as a refinement to improve those processes or problem areas where the solution is not known. But nearly 90 percent of your improvements can be driven through the concepts of Lean. This chapter begins by covering different ways businesses have elected to implement Lean.

I was first exposed to Lean in the late 1980s and have had the opportunity to introduce it in a number of settings. The concepts of cellular manufacturing are critical to Lean. In many cases, if the materials, tools, and equipment needed to produce and test a product are all kept in the same location, and arranged in a U-shaped pattern, products can be assembled and moved from bench to bench in a very efficient manner. If problems show up in the assembly, the assemblers are right next to where the error was made and can provide immediate feedback, quickly correcting problems before too many assemblies are completed incorrectly. The same can be said for an office environment. If the fulfillment process is process mapped, and if incidents of errors are captured and labeled in that map, you may have an opportunity to put two groups or functions together that need to be in communication to avoid the errors.

However, be sure to understand what you are taking apart before you make the changes. You may have two groups together that are in the same area so that they do communicate and there are no problems because of that arrangement. Make sure that moving them around will not make things worse. This is the advantage of using a team of people who do the day-to-day work to drive these changes. They recognize these issues and opportunities.

I've seen Lean introduced to a business through several different methods. I will cover the five approaches I've worked with or witnessed in driving Lean in businesses:

1. In a Heavy Industrial Setting

2. Self-Directed, Cross-Functional Work Teams
3. The Documented-Process Approach
4. The Leadership Team Approach
5. The Large *Kaizen*-Event Approach.

I have my preferences, but it's better for you to see these different situations. Some people have argued that Lean does not work in their business, and in many of those situations, I've then watched them successfully implement Lean.

Lean in a Heavy Industrial Setting

In the early 1990s, I was involved with a business that made high-voltage wire and cable. Most of the products produced could be run through four or five very large machines and then tested and shipped to the customer. Cables were ordered in different lengths that varied significantly among customers. They also had different specifications around extruded wall thicknesses of insulations. What was consistent was how most cable was assembled: always an insulation layer first, a semiconducting layer, a metal shield, and finally a plastic jacket. We recognized that our product was subjected to a tremendous amount of movement because the machines performing each of these processes were grouped by the process they performed, not the product they made. All the continuous vulcanization machines extruding rubber insulation on the wire were located in one building. The plastic extrusion lines were located in another building. This meant cable had to be trucked from building to building. That type of movement creates waste—unnecessary activity that could be eliminated to reduce cost. It took months—and in some cases years—but flow maps of the different products were produced, and machines were moved around to reduce the waste of unnecessary transportation so that an entire product could now be produced, tested, and shipped from one building. This is an important shift that many businesses make as they move to Lean. Their processes are now aligned to produce the product or service their customers' desire.

While the above is just a simple example of how Lean works, it was rather challenging applying Lean in a heavy industrial setting, where we moved different large machines, hundreds of feet long, into the same area. Nonetheless, the volume of product that was produced justified the moves by reducing handling, minimizing damage, and increasing throughput.

The Self-Directed, Cross-Functional Work Team

An electronic medical-device manufacturer was producing product using work orders. Here is a quick example of a work order: When they made product A, it had subassemblies B, C, and D, and raw materials or purchased parts E, F, and G. In the work orders system, items were purchased, sometimes inspected, and put into the stock room. When it was time to build the subassembly B, the parts were pulled out from the stockroom, put together in a kit, and moved though several departments in the factory for assembly. Operators in the factory charged their time to the work order. Once the assemblies were complete, they were put back in the stock room. Then they were pulled out on another work order, kitted, and sent through different departments in a factory to be assembled into product A, tested, and sent into finished-goods stock.

The cost and risk of damage with all that handling and movement adds unnecessary cost to the product. This medical-device manufacturer needed to shift to a Kanban Pull system. This also meant reconfiguring the layout of the factory floor and moving to U-shaped cells where the majority of the product assembly took place. But there was an added challenge: A failed attempt a few years earlier had left the business strongly believing that Lean or a Kanban Pull system would not work there.

 To make the needed changes happen, we organized four cross-functional, self-directed work teams to tackle the four most important issues the business was facing. Those four issues were:

1. The need for a streamlined manufacturing process
2. The need to reduce inventory by 50 percent
3. The need to get on-time customer deliveries up from 53 percent to over 99 percent
4. The need to electronically capture all medical-device information electronically.

These teams would have people from different functions, and each team would have an assigned leader, a scribe to capture minutes, and a facilitator. The leader was someone who had a vested interest in the success, or someone we felt was in an adjacent role who had great influencing skills that we hoped to develop and grow into a bigger role in the business. The scribe could be anyone, and the facilitator, who also functioned as a timekeeper to keep the meetings moving, was someone who could keep the team on track and not let them get sidelined on small issues. Every team was given a challenge—for example, an inventory reduction objective, or the goal of increasing throughput in the business by fifty percent.

We gave the teams two rules to follow. First, they could hire or fire anyone they wanted (but not the facilitator). This put an added pressure on the team. They did not want to get fired by their own peers! The second rule was that we required they present their accomplishments to the CEO one to three times, depending on the duration of the project. We would always give them three weeks' notice, but it was a big motivator. This ensured that they delivered results. One other important aspect was that we did not tell them up front, but when they completed their task successfully, we would disband the team, rewarding them with what was typically about $1,000 per participant. This was a nothing compared to the amount they saved the company with the changes they put in place. We also made sure that any changes were permanent, and the business would not slip back into its old inefficient habits.

So the four teams we created were:

1. The Work Order Elimination Team

2.   The Inventory Reduction Team
3.   The On Time Delivery Team
4.   The Quality Data Reporting Team.

Each of the teams was focused on three issues that were critical to the success of the business. And in the case of the Work Order Elimination team, they came back after wrestling with the challenge for two weeks and said, "You just want us to implement Lean." We said that we did, but we had wanted them to figure it out. Just as there is value in engaging the entire leadership team in strategic planning, there is tremendous value in this team approach as when they determine and implement a solution, they have a tremendous sense of ownership for the change. What is more effective than having a team of people viewed as respected leaders or informal leaders in multiple departments within the business solve a problem, and, at the same time, spread the word of the changes they are driving? This approach is infectious. The change is being driven from the lower levels of the organization. There is no better way to drive a cultural change in a business than to empower the people to drive changes, eliminating the problems suffered for years.

The teams were all very successful. In the case of the Work Order Elimination team, they introduced Lean in a section of one department, and within a few weeks, the whole department was converted to Lean. Then they moved to the next department, replicating their approach. It was quite a bit of work to create all the Kanban cards, but they often ordered in pizzas on the company's dime, and made Kanban cards while eating lunch together. In less than one year, the whole factory was converted to Lean. The inventory reduction team successfully halved the inventory, and the On-Time Delivery team improved on-time deliveries to 99 percent. The problems were fixed by the employees; they figured it out, and took great pride and ownership in the solution, making the results stick.

These self-directed cross-functional work teams are very powerful for solving general business problems, too. When I introduce Six Sigma, you will see how the problem-solving process is built around a team as well. Let me share a quick example of how these self-directed, cross-functional work teams are effective. A business made an oil-filled product that was used at high voltage. If the insulating oil leaked out, this very expensive product would be destroyed. This product was filled with oil in a heated environment, and then left to sit overnight on a piece of lint-free paper. If there were oil stains on the paper in the morning, the product had to be taken apart and fixed. For years, countless engineers tried to solve the problem with all sorts of technical solutions, with no success. When a self-directed, cross-functional team tackled the problem, they discovered something no one else ever considered. When the product was sealed, Vaseline was used to lubricate the o-ring that sealed the product—but different operators used different quantities of Vaseline. During the heating process, the Vaseline became a liquid that ultimately dripped off the product onto the lint-free paper. Defining the proper amount of Vaseline virtually eliminated the problem. In this case, the solution came from those assembling the product. I've seen many business problems solved with the self-directed, cross-functional team approach.

The Documented-Process Approach

After the medical-device factory was converted to Lean, a sister business in Florida needed help. When the concept of Lean was presented to them, they decided that they liked the concept of converting to Lean, but they wanted to hire their own people to drive Lean. They hired a couple of process engineers. They had been trained in Lean, and the approach they used was to build a value-stream map for every process in the business. These value-stream maps included a flow chart and labeling indicating what steps were value-added and what steps were non-value-added. Their work looked very professional, and they were very knowledgeable. But three fundamental problems became apparent with their approach. First, the value-stream maps were very detailed, adding significant time to the process and delaying the changes. They also were only useful until the process was changed; then all that work was discarded.

Second, by having process engineers make these maps independently and then direct all the changes, there was no engagement or empowerment of the employees who worked with the process every day. The business lost a tremendous opportunity to engage and empower the workforce in driving changes that would make their jobs easier, while giving them a sense of ownership that can be a great motivator.

The third issue was the total time it took to make all the changes. Not only did it take a long time to build the value-stream maps, but it took a longer time to train workers who had to learn the new process. Using the documented value-stream maps, it took them over a year to convert two product lines to Lean—and there were about twenty more product lines in that business. In our approach, with the self-directed work team, we converted an entire factory in less than twelve months, and it did more than twice the volume of business.

The Leadership Team Approach

This example of a Lean transformation took place in financial services. The business provided financing for commercial aircraft. In this business, there was a role referred to as the Quality Leader, whose job it was to define a deployment plan that targeted streamlining processes and improving the quality of the service provided. As this business had a centralized customer-fulfillment process that provided financing to customers and delivered aircraft for use, it was easy to build a process map depicting that core business process for a single aircraft transaction. It started with identifying financing opportunities in the marketplace, taking them through a funnel to assess their viability, and identifying those opportunities that had the best potential to be funded. Once a financing opportunity advanced to the stage where the customers liked the terms, Letters of Intent were signed. Next, the business providing the financing sent the details of the financing arrangement through a series of senior leaders for approval. Once they had the approval, they advised the customer of any changes to the Letter of Intent, moving forward once they had the customer's approval. A contract was then drafted from the Letter of Intent, negotiated, and signed. Finally the aircraft went through a preparation process and was delivered. Numerous points in the process presented opportunities for streamlining.

To attack the necessary changes, the core process was broken into sections, and a several senior leaders in the business were given the project of improving and streamlining their assigned section of the process. The head of sales was given the challenge of improving the conversion rate of opportunities up through getting a Letter of Intent. So if they were currently getting a Letter of Intent on two of every ten opportunities, his goal was to find out what could be done to increase that conversion rate to perhaps three or four Letters of Intent for every ten leads.

The president of the business chose to tackle the Letter of Intent process through to approval, working to reduce the number of days it took to get those internal approvals. The head of the legal department worked on optimizing the process from receiving the finalized and approved Letter of Intent through to getting the contract signed. And finally, the head of the technical group worked to streamline the delivery process to ensure meeting the committed delivery date. Each phase required a different approach.

The president was shocked to discover that lower-dollar-value financing opportunities took the longest to get approved. The reason? Since priority was always given to larger financing opportunities, the evaluations of these smaller financing opportunities were constantly interrupted. This proved very inefficient, because the evaluators had to reacquaint themselves with the smaller financing opportunities when they resumed working on them. This added unnecessary time to the process.

In the contract-signing phase, the challenge was not the time it took, but the bigger challenge was optimizing the length of the contract. By establishing an overall contract for each customer, and then creating an exception contract for each plane, the contract process flowed much faster.

In the delivery phase, analysis revealed that the delays primarily came from a certain type of aircraft transaction— something the company had never realized. By analyzing the deliveries by days early or late, and segmenting the results by the type of transaction, they identified one transaction type that accounted for more than 90 percent of all late deliveries. Now the problem could be corrected. The analysis allowed them to focus on improving the process for this transaction type, but it also allowed them to apply what they learned to the overall delivery performance.

It's an interesting exercise taking this type of approach, and it can be very informative for the senior leaders. In many ways, it's similar to the self-directed work team approach, since it engages and empowers those who touch the process daily, with the added benefit of improving morale. Presentations to the CEO can deliver the same unexpected discoveries, and allow the senior leaders to pursue more strategic issues.

The Large *Kaizen*-Event Approach

A final approach for driving a business transformation to a Lean approach is a large *Kaizen* event. *Kaizen* is a Japanese term commonly translated as "change for the good." Other businesses may not use the term *Kaizen* to describe the approach that is about to be described, but it operates by a similar process. The process culminates with thirty to forty people from all levels in the business meeting over a three- to ten-day period. The group lists every step of the current business process. This can be a process for taking orders, raising money for a financing opportunity, or delivering a service to a customer.

The group's next step is to identify the ideal process to be followed and what steps are needed to evolve the process to its ideal state. It takes about six weeks to plan properly for the event and several weeks of follow-up activity. The large face-to-face meeting begins with a few motivational speeches from the senior business leaders, all who having a vested interest in the process. At the end of the face-to-face meeting, the same senior leaders return to the room to hear the proposed changes. If there are specific needs, like investment in equipment or software changes, they can be presented to the leadership team at that point. In some cases, the proposed changes will include a specific request for the senior leaders to make an immediate go/no-go decision on any proposed investments. Normally, it would make sense to defer a decision like that until more data could be acquired, but an effectively functioning team should have been able to answer any questions that might be asked, allowing a final decision to be made. This type of immediate action is a powerful way to effect change.

A business was taking about eight days to set-up international customer accounts, when the process should have taken less than two days. We conducted an abbreviated *Kaizen*-type event where we pulled people together for three days and identified how to get the process of setting up the international customer's account down to just over one day. Given the short timeframe of the event, we got a green light to move forward, but had to submit the software change requests through the normal process, which resulted in the changes taking more than two years to implement.

However, tremendous value resulted from conducting the *Kaizen* event, as people who did the same job at different geographical locations in the business were able to learn how their peers were doing the same work more efficiently. They also were able to learn more about the process, which helped them better understand what the challenges were. The participants loved the session; they became aware of parts of the process they had never known existed. Everyone had a new appreciation for how others in the business were setting up accounts for international customers. The positive effects of this event were still being felt a year later as many of the people who attended still spoke very highly of the overall experience. Here again, the people selected were respected leaders or informal leaders of the groups they worked with, making them more effective in spreading the word on the changes that were being delivered.

TIM WOOD

One tool for tackling Lean is known by the acronym, *TIM WOOD*. Making the acronym a name makes it easier to remember. TIM WOOD stands for the wastes that exist in processes today: Transportation, Inspection, Motion, Waiting, Overproduction, Over-processing, and Defects. Transportation refers to the needless movement of material or components. Inspection involves unnecessary quality checks that should be done by the people performing the process. Motion involves excess walking or reaching to get parts or components to assemble an item, or having to walk to other departments to get information that should be readily available in this group. Waiting involves people who become unproductive waiting for information or materials to process. Overproduction involves the manufacturing of material or information not currently needed, which will now have to be stored. Over-processing involves performing unnecessary work, like painting parts that are not visible. Defects are flaws in a product that make it unacceptable to the customer. Training team members on the TIM WOOD acronym helps them remember what they are trying to eliminate.

5S

The abbreviation *5S* also helps organizations implement Lean. It stands for five words that begin with the letter *S* in Japanese that were used to help businesses organize any work area to maximize efficiency. The five English words that are typically used today are *Straighten, Sort, Standardize, Shine,* and *Sustain.* I have also seen *Safety* informally included as a sixth *S*.

> *Straighten* means that everything is assigned a place and is returned there after it is used. These items are positioned at the best point of use.

> *Sort* means to keep only the items needed in the workspace and remove those that are not necessary or that can interfere with work.

> *Standardize* requires that work practices be defined and followed consistently. Each work station where the same task is performed should be set up identically, so anyone can easily move between stations.

> *Shine* suggests just what it implies: Keep the work area clean and orderly. At the end of the day, the work area should be given a final cleaning.

> *Sustain* refers to diligently maintaining the first four Ss and continuing to review all work areas for improvements.

End-State Vision

Now that I've described the different approaches for implementing Lean, you may have noticed that they are all tactical. Many businesses implementing Lean may not have taken the time to develop a strategic view, but it's critical that an end-state vision exists of how the business will look when Lean has been fully implemented. That may be one, three, or five years down the road, depending on the business.

I had a great interaction with a hospital that was midstream on implementing Lean. That had employed a lot of great tactical changes being driven by all levels of the organization while meeting their savings numbers, but their major concern was that they operated in a very unique environment. This hospital did not have their doctors as employees, but the doctors were contractors that billed their patients directly. The hospital was paid by the patients' insurance companies for providing the operating rooms and recovery rooms. This created an unusual arrangement in which their doctors were also customers in their processes. As opportunities were studied to streamline their operating rooms, doctors who had unique requests regarding their preferred instruments introduced significant variability, making it harder to standardize instruments in the operating room.

The hospital's biggest challenge, however, centered around taking a strategic view of what they were trying to accomplish. Since they had hit the first year's savings target and felt they were in good shape to hit the second year's number, they were pretty confident about their progress. But they also had some large-scale opportunities which, if they did not take some initial steps today, they would not be able to act upon when they had the resources to focus on them in the future. In some cases, they might have to propose regulatory changes now, to get them approved in time for the hospital to devote resources to making the change in the following year.

This just further emphasizes the need for the end-state vision. If the person leading the Lean movement does not have a defined vision, then there may be a need to take the strategic planning approach to define the vision and determine the right course of action. Interviewing the key leaders individually, then gathering them for an offsite meeting to define the overall Lean strategy may be the best way to get the needed buy-in and define the multiyear go-forward plan. I'm hesitant to use the word multiyear, because these changes need to be driven as quickly as possible, but if regulatory changes are required, the longer timeframe may be a reality. Most businesses without regulatory restrictions should target implementing Lean in less than one year.

Another point had to do with the doctors not being employees and acting more like customers. Doctors are often stereotyped as a difficult group to impose change upon, but they are no different from any other group of people. Some of them would welcome change, some would be neutral to change, and the rest of them might oppose change. Identifying doctors who are open to change and implementing changes with them makes it easier to attract the subgroup of neutral doctors.

Successful Lean programs drive changes that increase *throughput*—the number of items or patients processed per unit of time. In a hospital setting, this can translate into increased availability of operating rooms and other hospital facilities, which can create a very positive impact on the income of the doctors who work with the changes. So now a streamlined operating room may be able to perform twenty-four surgeries each week, versus only eighteen surgeries under the old operating model. This can be a very powerful way to persuade more doctors to accept the new Lean, streamlined approach. Starting with those who are cooperative to pilot the new approach and share the beneficial results is a great strategy for engaging any group of people who may be resistant to change.

Again, do not underestimate the importance of having an end-state vision and an overall strategy when implementing Lean. You are now aware of several tactical methods that can help as you look to streamline processes. Every situation is going to be different and may require a variation of the above approaches. Given the option, I'm a strong advocate for using the self-directed, cross-functional team made up of respected formal and informal leaders from across the relevant departments in the business. And I recommend that you try to implement your Lean changes as quickly as possible.

7

SUPPLY CHAIN MANAGEMENT

What supply chain management means to one person, may be very different to the next person. It depends on where the person is in the overall process of supplying the good or service. If the person works in retail, supply chain management is everything leading up to the item appearing on the rack for sale. If the person works for a manufacturing firm selling to a distributor, then her view of the supply chain is everything leading up to the purchased parts and components arriving at the point of use in the manufacturing process rather than the retailer's point of sale.

When shifting any manufacturing business over to Lean, it's critical to manage the supply chain effectively. A conversion to Lean begins with converting the factory to Lean, but the vendors play such a critical role that they need to be engaged in the process as soon as possible. Creating an Inventory Reduction team that partners with the Purchasing team to work with vendors to take back inventory, or sell inventory, or find ways to modify the inventory for other uses, is vital. Introducing preventative measures to avoid having the inventory grow again is important. The Purchasing department will play a vital role in managing the inventory in the future. There are several methods of material delivery to consider. Below are several examples of successful changes that can create savings for many businesses.

The Breadman Routine

Imagine that the cardboard boxes the product was packed in were purchased from half a dozen vendors and were often bought as a three-year supply to get the lowest price. Think about the cost of occupying all that shelf space in the storeroom for years. Should demand for the product packed in those boxes drop, the large inventory of boxes could grow to a four-, five-, or six-year supply. Over time, those boxes could get damaged and become unusable. Consolidating purchase of cardboard boxes to one vendor who will send a driver every other day to replace boxes taken from dedicated storage racks in the Shipping Department (so cardboard retrieval is self-serve) benefits both vendor and customer. The cardboard vendor receives all the business and helps the customer by assuming the inventory management role. This type of partnering is the way a world-class company needs to operate.

Any business with an inventory stockroom filled with boxes is paying a huge, hidden cost. The company's employees have to unload those boxes from a truck, pack them in the storeroom, and enter them into the computer as inventory. The boxes may have to be moved them from time to time, or they might get wet from a leaky roof, or get damaged by a forklift. And this is not to mention the square footage of floor space they are occupying. When the boxes run out, a purchase order must be issued, and the process must be repeated. This is a lot of effort to expend for a process that could easily be turned over to a vendor.

In a similar approach, all the hardware—nuts, bolts, and screws—can be moved from the stockroom and all stored on a wall of the main production floor. When hardware is needed, an assembler would take a bag and bring it to the production cell. Just like the cardboard supplier, a driver from the hardware supplier could come in twice a week to check the stock of hardware, replenishing any bins that were low. We refer to this process for delivering the cardboard and the hardware as the "Breadman Routine." Just as the breadman restocks the shelves with bread in the grocery store, vendors can do the same thing with their products. In both cases, the driver reviews the delivery with the appropriate supervisor, and the vendor would send a bill based on what was delivered.

The In-House Store

In this example, circuit-board components were sourced from multiple vendors, and were consolidated down to two. Since one vendor managed the vast majority of the parts, they were provided a locked cage on our factory floor where the vendor-owned inventory was stored. But instead of issuing a purchase order, the machine operators would drop Kanban cards on the table outside the cage. The supplier had a driver come in every day or every other day to set out the parts we needed. It's also worth noting that we allowed the vendor to store parts in that cage that they provided to other customers in the same industrial park. The vendor greatly appreciated that option as they could be more responsive to that customer, too.

In converting the factory to Lean, we saw a significant increase in our throughput. Entire subassemblies were no longer sent to the stockroom, and parts were delivered directly to the point of use. With these changes, the typical time between when we started building the monitor circuit boards to when we shipped that board out as part of a finished monitor was reduced from twelve weeks to less than five days. We set up forty-five-day payment terms with our vendors. Since our collection terms were thirty days for our monitors, the circuit board components, like many other parts, became a virtual inventory. *We were able to use the parts in the products we shipped, but paid for them with the money we took in for selling them in the assembled state.*

Ordering Parts from the Factory Floor

Finally, as this was occurring in the late 1990s, a fax server played a critical role in running this business. For many of the fabricated components, arrangements were made with vendors to provide any component within 48 hours. We provided vendors with a forecast that was updated monthly, so when an assembler on the floor scanned the barcode on the Kanban card, a message was sent to a fax server to fax an order for the Kanban lot size of that part to the vendor. The vendor was required to deliver the parts, within 48 hours, directly to the shop floor. Today's advanced technology allows this to happen with no fax server. Scanning the barcode sends the message to the vendor and a copy to the buyer in purchasing, to allow for any required verification.

Our successes led to our helping other businesses, both within our company and in the state of Connecticut. We worked to help convert a sister business in Germany to Lean. We took our German colleagues to meet with our vendors and showed them how the vendors managed our inventory. At first they were in disbelief; they could not believe that vendors would accept these terms. But within six months, their vendors were beginning to do the same thing.

We also learned something else in that process: Our vendors were holding three to six months of finished goods inventory for us, when they should only have been holding about one month's worth. This was a cost issue for them. If a part-change notice came through, there would be an added cost to rework those finished parts. So we brought them into our factory and taught them how to implement Lean in their shops. They loved it, and it just made our working relationship that much stronger. In fact, we had a vendor whose building burned to the ground, but they never missed a shipment to our business. That vendor understood the value of their customers, and had contingency plans and similar Kanban Pull arrangements with their suppliers, so they were able to supply the parts without interruption.

These vendor-customer relationships can be taken to any level. I'm aware of several businesses today that will have vendors quote a part for the life of the product they produce. Think about the advantages this creates for both parties. It provides a consistent stream of business for the supplier, and now that a partnering relationship exists, the supplier will often initiate and provide the customer some ideas for reducing the cost of a part. This benefits both the customer and the supplier; the customer reduces its costs, and the supplier builds goodwill with the customer that often leads to more part contracts.

Consider the traditional customer-supplier relationship, where the customer frequently gets multiple quotes from several suppliers and then plays one supplier against the other to get to the lowest price. If a supplier provides a cost-reduction idea to the customer, what is to stop the customer from modifying the part specification and having the other suppliers incorporate that same change to help get to the lowest price? While this dedicated-vendor approach does require checks and balances, it builds the right type of relationship between a customer and a supplier. It's important to agree that the pricing is going to be validated periodically by having different vendors quote the part. If one of the quoted suppliers comes in with a lower price, it creates an opportunity to explore whether that savings can be achieved with the existing vendor. But this approach should be communicated to the supplier up front, so they understand how the process works. High-quality suppliers will often recognize the value of the relationship and not allow themselves to be undercut by a lower cost supplier.

Other Applications for this Concept

Certain types of service businesses can realize similar benefits from partnering with their suppliers. Any time you are dependent on a supplier to provide you a physical component, you should consider how the process can operate in the most efficient manner and work with your supplier to get to that ideal state. You can also apply this logic in financial services. Consider a business that lends money and in many cases may need to source that money. These businesses often have their own treasury group that provides the money to make a loan to another business. Some of the smaller commercial lending businesses may not have that luxury, so they may have to partner with different banks to provide funding. Selecting a preferred supplier offering a key contact to help streamline the communication and provide rate information at a moment's notice can help improve the precision with which you price those deals and minimize unexpected changes that can affect your customer.

Supply-Chain Risk

The last element of managing the supply chain that I want to touch on is supply-chain risk. I mentioned earlier about the great supplier relationship we had with one supplier; when their factory suffered a fire, they never skipped a beat on deliveries. That may not always be the case. Numerous factors can disrupt a supply chain: weather/geological anomalies, raw material shortages, and even the financial performance of the vendor's business. While we have very little control over these factors, there are ways of assessing the risks of each of these factors, and in some cases there may be ways of getting early indicators of the financial health of each vendor. If a part has a very limited supply base or requires a raw material that could fall into short supply, alternate strategies should be explored. This may include increasing your internal stock based on historic periods of short supply. In terms of financial performance, several companies exist that provide an alternate rating methodology to what the Big Three credit-rating agencies provide. Engaging one of these firms can help you assess the financial health of your vendors, and if early indicators of potential problems arise, you can proactively discuss the situation with the vendor and decide whether you are comfortable with them as a sole supplier.

In summary, properly managing your supply chain can provide a valuable competitive advantage over your competition by lowering your costs through reducing inventory and eliminating unnecessary handling. The resulting increased throughput and improved flow of material will also improve your own customers' experiences.

8

STATISTICAL PROCESS CONTROL

This sounds a lot more complicated than it is. In any process, data can be collected and plotted using *Statistical Process Control* to let the business know if a problem is *about* to occur.

Let me begin by providing a practical example of how Statistical Process Control can work. Back in the late 1980s, we were learning about Lean, and many of us were getting trained in how to implement Lean and Statistical Process Control. As an example, we observed an auto manufacturer who had two automatic-transmission suppliers—one in Ohio and one in Japan. When studying data around warranty repairs, the factory in Ohio was found to have a much higher rate of returns, as much as three or four times that of the factory in Japan. What made it interesting was that both factories were building *identical* transmissions. When the engineers took the transmissions apart to study the differences, they discovered a problem with the tolerances on the parts.

Let me explain that more: A *tolerance* is a predefined range of measurements that a part must meet. So let's say we are making super balls. We may be making super balls that are one inch in diameter, but we have to define a tolerance around that diameter. Given that it does not need to be very exact, we would say the super ball should be more than 0.925" and less than 1.075"in diameter. That represents the acceptable range for the size of these super balls, and it is written as 1.000" ± 0.075". Please note that the ± symbol means "plus or minus."

Number of Parts Above or Below Tolerance

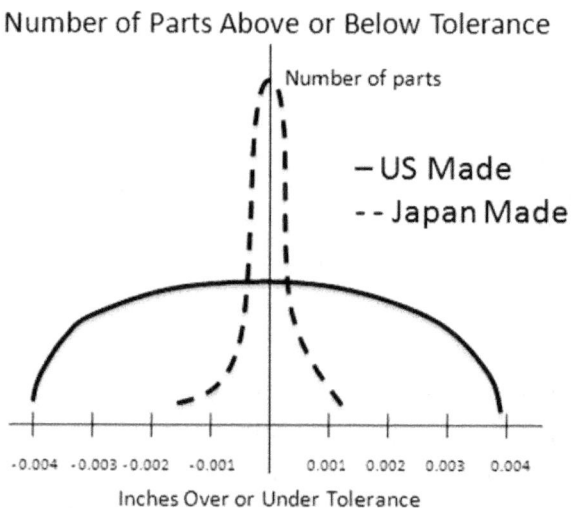

Inches Over or Under Tolerance

In the case of the auto transmissions, there are many, many parts inside of the transmission, and the tolerances are much tighter. For example, on the 0.125" steel plate that presses against the clutch plates, the tolerance might be $\pm$ 0.004 inches. What they saw in the Japanese transmissions was that the Japanese parts were holding the majority of these tolerances to $\pm$ 0.001 inches, while the US parts were holding their tolerances to the full range of $\pm$ 0.004 inches. This meant the US-built transmissions, built with parts that were on the high end of that range, were too tight, and this caused them to wear out faster. The picture on the previous page provides a visual of what I've just described. The parts were all measured and the vertical axis represents the count of parts with the tolerance listed on the x-axis. You can see the tighter tolerance on the Japanese parts produced fewer defects in the transmissions.

The issue is variability in a process. The objective of Lean is to streamline processes and eliminate variability. Statistical Process Control charts can be introduced to keep processes in control and to keep Lean processes flowing in a timely manner.

Within a few months of learning about Statistical Process Control, I was invited to join a team of people to visit a vendor making aluminum housings. I travelled with the purchasing contact and two senior quality-control leaders. We visited a large-scale machine shop, and it was unlike any machine shop I had visited. The place was spotless, and every worker seemed to take incredible care with keeping their work space neat and orderly. The lathes, vertical milling stations, and drill presses ran continuously. What I found very impressive was that every machine operator who produced parts was manually measuring the critical dimensions and plotting them on a Statistical Process Control chart. Each operator understood control charts and knew how to complete and interpret a control chart. Even the workers who spoke very little English were able to complete and interpret the data patterns on the chart. Checking the quality of the part at the point of creation and having the machine operator be accountable for that level of quality is the best way to make the best possible product you can produce. These machine operators were detecting and solving problems that they never would have been able to detect later in the process. The machine operators made adjustments when they saw trends and anomalies on the charts and avoided creating unacceptable parts.

Another example of Statistical Process Control concerns a manufacturer who made circuit boards. The circuit boards were coated with flux, a material that helped clean the metal parts and allowed the solder to flow better when the boards went through an automated soldering machine. Since that flux was conductive, it could damage the boards so the residual flux had to be cleaned off. There was a deionized water washing machine that would clean off the flux. After the machine washed too many boards, the water became too conductive and would damage the boards. To determine if the water became too conductive, the water in the machine was tested daily. The data was recorded on a control chart that was displayed on the machine. If the conductivity of the water became too high, the water would be changed. The threshold for failing the conductivity test was below the level that would damage the boards, so even if the water was too conductive, any boards processed with that failed water were not damaged. This also did not stop the flow of production. The water was then changed and the machine resumed operation. This tracking engaged the operator and empowered them to stop the production line to maintain a high quality product.

Statistical process control can be applied in any industry, including financial services. Items that can be tracked include variation from deliver date, time to decision, time to fund, and time to onboard new clients. These are just a few of many possible measurements. It comes down to what the business sees as being worthwhile to track.

The *control chart* is a great tool for one additional reason. Every time operators enter a value on the chart, it's a reminder to operators that they are accountable for the quality of the product or process they are tracking. That is a powerful way to get people to take ownership over the quality of the product they are producing or the service they are delivering.

9

DATA DISTRIBUTIONS AND SIX SIGMA

Many people who have heard of Six Sigma know that it began with Motorola. Soon Allied Signal adopted it, and then, in 1995, it came to GE. Six Sigma is a problem-solving methodology that can help businesses identify and correct problems using data. Many businesses work off the opinions or anecdotes of trusted experts when trying to identify solutions to their business problems. I've seen too many situations where the expert was contradicted by data that was gathered and analyzed. This approach can be a powerful tool for any business.

Before I get into explaining Six Sigma, we need to have a consistent understanding of what a distribution of data looks like. By distribution, I mean a distribution of data. Every year in the late summer on the Long Island Sound, there is a Bluefish Tournament with a $25,000 prize for the person who catches the heaviest bluefish—not bad for a day out on the boat!

But there is also a rule that if the fish caught is less than twenty-eight inches long, it must be released back into the sound. There are thousands of fishermen who participate in this weekend tournament. The winner is the person who catches the heaviest fish, and it usually weighs around sixteen pounds. If we were to have every fisherman write down how many fish he caught and how long in inches they were, we would have a vast distribution of data on fish lengths. It's estimated that there are over 3,000 boats in the competition. If we assume that each boat catches eight to twelve fish a day, for two days, there should be over 60,000 fish caught. The length of these fish could vary in length from as small as fifteen inches to almost forty inches. If we plotted them, with the Y-axis being count of fish caught at a given length, and the X-axis being the length of the fish, we would have a distribution of bluefish lengths in Long Island Sound. This is depicted in the figure below.

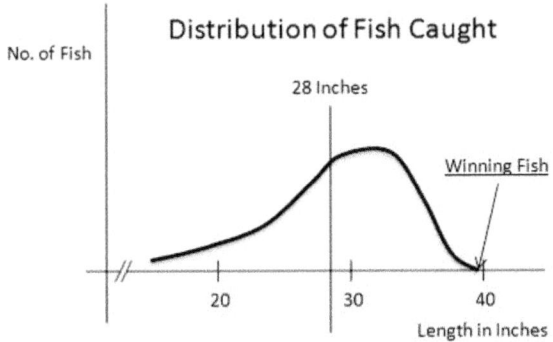

We have also added our measurement of quality, in that the

fish must be longer than twenty-eight inches, or it is a defect. From these numbers, we can calculate a Sigma value, or the count of standard deviations within which this process performs. To take it a step further, let's say we had 100 fishermen who did not catch a single fish less than twenty-eight inches long. What could be causing that? Is it where they fished? The depth they fished at? The type of bait they used?

This is how Six Sigma can help us solve our business's problems. Put simply, by studying those that perform better than anyone else, we can study what they did differently, and use that to improve everyone else's performance.

10

SIX SIGMA PROJECTS

So now that we have a common definition of what a distribution is, let's talk about Six Sigma. The name Six Sigma has often generated confusion for those who are not familiar with what it means. As mentioned before, a Sigma is a standard deviation, and if your process or product meets the customer specification at a level of Six Sigma, or it runs within six standard deviations, this translates to a process creating less than 3.4 defects for every million items or events.

The best way to think about it is to consider processes that require manual inputs from people. At their best, these processes tend to run around three sigma—meaning that about 99 percent of what they produce is acceptable.

People make mistakes. Six Sigma represents a target. It may or may not be attainable, so the question you always have to ask is, "Is going for that incremental improvement in performance worth the investment?"

It depends. A good Six Sigma project will improve a process performance, and it may only go from 2.5 Sigma to 4.0 Sigma. In some cases, the cost to the business to improve the process performance above 4.0 Sigma, or a yield of 99.38 percent, may exceed the value of the savings generated by operating at a more defect-free level.

So Six Sigma is really about performing improvement projects within your business to drive process, product, and/or service improvements. Let me give a few examples of how a Six Sigma project works.

Equipment Financing Example

I once worked with a business involved in providing equipment financing to companies. Let's say a company had to buy a printing press or a forklift, or perhaps a machine that takes grease off large metal parts, and it does not want to tie up their current holdings of cash to pay for the machine. This equipment-financing company had sales people who called on these business CFOs and offered them financing options to pay for the equipment. It provided an alternate source from the bank, and it often provided a lower cost to the CFO. The equipment-financing company had a business leader who wanted to grow the top line of his business, so we suggested doing a Six Sigma project around improving his sales team's performance.

The best way to think about a Six Sigma project is that you have a practical problem you turn into a statistical problem.

You find a statistical solution for this problem, and then turn this into a practical solution. So in our equipment-lending business, our practical problem was that we wanted to increase our sales, or the dollar value of equipment loans being made. We needed to turn that into a statistical problem, and we could only do that by finding the right way to measure it. In this case, we chose to measure volume per sales rep per quarter. The business had a few thousand sales reps, and we were able to collect five years of data.

For each sales rep, we also collected information on factors. We found out things such as how many years they had been in sales, how many years they'd been in sales at the current company, how physically large their territory was, and how large it was in terms of population. We researched what level of education these sales rep had, how long they had been in their territories, how many miles they put on their company cars, whether they had ever worked in the underwriting group that evaluated and approved each financing deal, and how many target companies were estimated to be in their territory.

When selecting factors to look at, pick factors that you can both measure and take action upon. For example, determining if the sales volume is statistically higher for sales reps in cities, versus those in suburban or rural areas, may not be helpful. You can't put all the sales reps in cities, can you? But it could tell you that you may get more benefits from adding additional sales reps in cities. That factor only addresses the actionable piece. For the factor to be measureable, make sure you can get data on that factor. You may think you can find out how many years the reps spent at different companies or competitors, but the company's human resources records may not have that level of detail. It's very important to consider these two elements when selecting factors.

Back to the project example, we next collected data and ran statistical tests on twenty to thirty factors.

Why statistical tests? Statistical tests can tell you if two groups of numbers actually can be considered different. So for example, we realized that we could take the sales-volume-per-rep-per-quarter number and test to see if the better-performing sales reps had factors in common. Perhaps we would discover that they all had at least fifteen years with their current company, or that they all worked in big cities.

Finding out what factors correlate to better employee performance can help you find a way to teach other employees to take similar approaches, therefore helping to grow the business. At the equipment-leasing company, we collected data on twenty to thirty different factors, and tests were conducted on all of them. What stood out for this company was that the sales reps who had worked in the underwriting group had better performance statistically than those who had not. It appeared that the sales reps who understood what criteria were important to consider when lending money to businesses performed statistically better than those that did not have that background. So now we had our statistical solution.

Here it's critical to remember that *correlation* does not mean *causation*. Just because two things correlate, this does not mean that one causes the other. For example, if I told you that the number of crimes correlates directly with the number of churches in every city in the United States, you might be surprised. But that correlation is dependent on the number of people in a given area. More people means there are more churches, and more people also means there are more crimes. Another example might be ice-cream sales and drowning. When ice-cream sales go up, so does the frequency of drowning. So, should we stop selling ice cream? Of course not. Ice cream sales do not cause drowning; but the hot weather brings out more swimmers, including inexperienced swimmers who are more likely to drown. The same hot weather causes more people to purchase and eat ice cream. Both events are correlated, but one is not causing the other.

In our case, we had identified a *correlation* between whether or not a sales rep had worked in the underwriting group, but we needed to make sure that there was *causation.* Was it correct to interpret that people who worked in the underwriting group had higher sales *because* they understood the underwriting requirements better? Or could it be due to something else? For instance, maybe the people who now worked in the underwriting group knew the sales reps who had worked there before, and were more likely to approve their deals because they personally knew and trusted them.

All alternative possibilities need to be considered. Many people make the mistake of assuming that a *correlation* means there is *causation.* The way to test for *causation* is to run a *pilot* to test the proposed solution. In an ideal scenario, the changes are tested on a portion of the group, while the rest of the group does not change their process. This allows for comparisons between the two current performances and also a comparison between the previous performances.

Fortunately, in the case of the equipment-lending business, running a pilot program was easy to do. Every summer, the company hired about thirty new sales reps, so an underwriting training module was developed and introduced to the class. In an ideal setting, half the class would have been trained, and the other half would function as a control group. Then after they worked for a year originating loans, the performance of each half of the class could have been compared.

In this case, the entire class was trained, so we could not compare untrained-rookie reps with trained rookie reps. We could, however, compare the first-year sales statistics of the trained class with the first-year sales statistics generated by previous, untrained classes. We also discovered that the sales figures of the underwriting-trained first-year reps were statistically closer to those of the experienced sales reps. Now we had a practical solution.

So, to summarize, the equipment-lending company had a *practical problem:* its desire to increase sales volume. We turned this into a *statistical problem* by choosing to measure the quarterly volume of sales per rep. Through analyzing the information we found a *statistical solution,* which indicated that sales reps with experience in the underwriting group had higher sales. Finally, through a pilot, we were able to demonstrate that sales reps with underwriting training performed better than those who were not trained, and in fact, their numbers were closer to those generated by experienced sales reps.

While this was a good example of how a project should work, the amount of time it took was challenging. A Six Sigma project is best done in six months or less, because it's important to solve the problem and deliver the financial gains quickly. Since this was a business-wide project and it was dependent on the once-a-year hiring of a new class of sales reps, it took nearly two years. But it helped drive some top-line improvement in the business.

All good projects should follow the Practical Problem, Statistical Problem, Statistical Solution, Practical Solution approach. Ideally, a Six Sigma project is solving a problem with no known solution. But when a solution is already known, a Six Sigma project can confirm that it is the right one.

A Venture Finance Lending and Leasing Example

Another example of a great Six Sigma project involved a lending-and-leasing business where an internal reorganization had all investment approvals reporting into a different final approver. This final approver was more risk adverse than his predecessor and was not comfortable providing equipment loans to companies that had not yet turned a profit and were operating in the latter stages of the new venture cycle. In this case, the *practical problem* was a very low deal-approval rate or a very low conversion rate.

Since these companies were not cash-flow positive yet, they were dependent on another round of equity funding to ultimately pay off the loan or lease provided. When selecting what to measure, a discrete measurement was chosen: whether the deal had lost money. It is discrete, in that the either was a loss, or not. This can be compared against the continuous measure of quarterly volume per rep that we used in the previous example. This discrete metric was the *statistical problem*—whether or not the deal lost money. The logic was that if we could determine what caused deals not to lose money, the business could target those types of deals, and then improve its conversion rate.

Data was collected from all the deals completed over an eight-year period. The data set included deals that were funded and deals that were not funded. Among the factors tested were the size of company, venture sponsors, stage of life, equity-to-debt ratio, round of funding, industry, and year of inception. In that process, one thing that surprised everyone was the discovery that deals with a higher ratio of equity to debt (more equity, less debt) lost money more than deals with less equity and more debt, and the difference was statistically significant. When we questioned the experts on the findings, they were surprised, but it made them realize that there was something else we should be looking at in the evaluation stage. When deal performance was plotted against the amount of cash the company burned each month, a threshold appeared, separating very-good performance from very-poor performance. Also, there was a difference in the performance of deals at certain stages of the venture cycle. So here we found our *statistical solution.*

Finally, a pilot needed to be run to test the solution, which turned out to be a revised set of underwriting criteria. The problem was that all the data in the history of the business was used to analyze the problem. Ideally, 60 percent should have been used for analysis, and then two groups of 20 percent should have been held back to verify the results. Anytime you analyze a set of data, you cannot use the same data used to come up with the results to validate the results. So this meant another sample of historical deals was needed to test the proposed underwriting criteria.

Rather serendipitously, the business had made a recent acquisition that included a company performing the same type of lending and leasing to early-stage companies. Old data files were accessed, and a spreadsheet was built to match the original data set, using approximately forty deals done in the same timeframe. Keep in mind that while eight years of data was collected, the last three years could not be used, because the outcome of those deals was not yet known. There was still time for recent deals to fail, but deals older than three years had all been repaid or had lost money. When we applied the revised evaluation parameters to the recent acquisition's deals, we discovered that the ratio of deals performing well versus those performing poorly rose from slightly over 40 percent to 90 percent. This was the *practical solution*, as it confirmed the new underwriting model should significantly reduce the approval of deals that will ultimately lose money.

Using these results, we produced a summary of the analysis and presented our findings to the senior leaders who were hesitant to commit. Leaders in favor of the business were also in the room to provide political support. The senior leaders could not argue with the data presented, and they agreed to implement the changes. The changes were implemented, and the deal-approval rate went up significantly.

One of the best ways to understand how to apply Six Sigma is to review successful projects. With that in mind, below are two more examples of projects that should be helpful.

A Call Center Example

A business had a customer call center. Given that it was a call center, performance statistics were tracked and reported regularly. In the case of this call center, a key statistic was customer wait time. The business had targeted that 90 percent of the calls should be answered in sixty seconds or less. They were actually running in the low 60-percent range and needed to raise the number by 30 percent. This information provided both the *practical* and *statistical problems* together. The *practical problem* was the need to answer customer calls faster. The *statistical problem* was to improve the percentage of calls answered in less than a minute from just over 60 percent to over 90 percent. This was a discrete measure; if the call was answered in less than one minute, it was listed as acceptable. If the call was answered in more than a minute; it was listed as a defect.

Data on this process was collected and analyzed. Areas studied included individual performance, team performance, and certain demographics about the customers who might call in. We discovered that this call center had groups of people assigned to take calls by client type, or by the types of investment products. In analyzing the types of calls, we noted that some client groups were understaffed, and some of the product groups were overstaffed. Here a statistically different performance by groupings was discovered. And this turned out to be the *statistical solution*.

The decision was made to reorganize the groups from twelve teams to just three. One of those subteams would have over 80 percent of the call center staff in it, because it had the largest volume of product calls. Since there was no practical way to pilot this change, the decision was made to make these changes across the entire group. The changes were made, and within the first week, the call center met its target of answering 90 percent of its calls in the first minute. At the beginning of this project, the head of the call center was prepared to submit a request to increase headcount by nearly 20 percent. The request was not submitted, and generated significant cost avoidance for the business. The call center group has continued to meet its 90-percent target.

As you likely have noticed, the first three examples provided showed the application of Six Sigma in a non-manufacturing setting. That is intentional. In my experiences, it is easy to apply Six Sigma in a manufacturing environment, because there is a significant amount of data, and it's perceived as being easier to gather and analyze. But all the data you need to create a Six Sigma solution is available in *any* business. You just need to engage the right people who are open to working hard to gather and validate the data and then keep an open mind during the analysis phase.

An International Shipments Example

For a final project, we will look at a manufacturer who was tracking its on-time delivery to all of its customers. The on-time delivery numbers were up in the 99-percent range; however the vast majority of the shipments were domestic. The head of the shipping department decided to look at the international shipments, since they had a higher percentage of late shipments. This defined our *practical problem:* late shipments to international customers.

When the shipping and stores manager reviewed the late shipments, he decided to measure the count of late shipments per month, and this became his *statistical problem.*

He gathered data on product shipments, the country the shipments went to, whether it was shipped with accessories, the week of the month it shipped in (later in the month, there were more shipments), the shipping clerk that processed the order, the customer service representative who took the order, the method of shipment, and several other factors. When he conducted statistical tests on all these factors, what proved to be statistically significant was which customer service representative had booked the order. There were five representatives, who were authorized to book international orders, but two of them were more senior, and all of their shipments went out on time. The other three were more junior, and all three had the late shipments. This gave him his *statistical solution.*

His next step was interviewing the group to understand why some did well and others did not. He discovered that the two senior reps had received training in how to process international orders that the three junior members had never received. Rather than pilot the solution by only training one member and seeing if that person performed better, the decision was made to train all three representatives. Data was then collected over the next three months. Here he had the *practical solution.* After collecting three months of data, the manager discovered that all five reps were performing the same, and the problem had been resolved.

Let's take a moment to reconsider these examples. The first project took over eighteen months to complete. The second project took fifteen months to complete. The call center project took just over five months to complete, and the last project was done in five months. The scope of each project discussed here was narrower than the one preceding it; the project in the first example impacted the entire business; the fourth example directly affected only a few departments. The first two projects were higher-level projects or Master Black Belt- and Black Belt-level projects. The last two were lower-level projects or Green Belt projects.

Let me make one other point on what I define as the *statistical problem* in a project. Some Six Sigma experts will argue that the *statistical problem* is when the factors are collected and the statistical tools are used in the project. I intentionally identify it as the point when the right measurement is selected for the project. It makes it much easier for the students of Six Sigma to understand. Six Sigma can be complex and intimidating; making it simple makes it easier to apply.

11

SIX SIGMA BELTS AND TRAINING

I will start with the simplest and go to the most complex when describing the belts.

Green Belt Certification

To get a Green Belt certification, the candidate must attend training, take a test, and complete a project. This is typical, but may vary from company to company.

Black Belt and Master Black Belt Certification

To get a Black Belt certification, the candidate must attend an advanced training course, take a tougher test, and complete two large projects. In some cases, a Black Belt may have to work fulltime for a certain period of time doing improvement projects to get certification. Finally, to get a Master Black Belt certification, the candidate must go through the same certification as the Black Belt, but also must mentor any combination of ten projects that can be Green Belt or Black Belt projects.

Two other levels of certification that exist are a Quality Leader and an alternate color belt—often yellow or white, though I've heard of several variations.

The Quality Leader Certification

The Quality Leader is the senior role and is responsible for defining the strategy and deployment of Six Sigma in the business. If a Quality Leader is going to be certified, he or she must first attend the advanced training, pass the advanced test, complete a Six Sigma project, and submit a deployment plan for approval. Quality Leaders may be called on to certify Master Black Belts in some businesses.

Finally, the alternate belt colors tend to be introductory to Six Sigma. Very short training and a very simplified project are required for certification. While I've never certified anyone at that level, some firms like the quick strike of a small, abbreviated project.

Let me take a moment to mention how the Quality Leader role can be very valuable to the business. The Quality Leader defines the Six Sigma deployment plan in a business. He or she needs to understand and anticipate the strategic direction of the business, and needs to be engaged in the strategic-planning process. When the deployment plan is created, it should target the core business process. From a high-level map, areas are identified where opportunities exist for improvement. Does the business need help on lead generation, or improving on-time delivery of a product or service? Does the business need to improve collections, or is there a part of the process that is a bottleneck for processing product? Identifying these opportunities helps the Quality Leader recognize necessary tactical improvements. If the Strategic Plan of the business targets growing into an adjacent space, the deployment plan should identify how the Six Sigma team will collaborate with the business to support or lead those changes.

Six Sigma: It's About the Process

Now that you understand the different belts and how projects are conducted, the next step is to give a quick overview of the steps necessary to get the results. As in many areas of life, if you focus on the process, you do not have to worry about the outcome. When students learn to study effectively, building their knowledge through a consistent daily study routine, cramming for exams disappears. All great Six Sigma projects are based on that theory in business. If you follow the defined steps of Six Sigma—in other words, if you properly apply the Six Sigma process—you will not have to worry about the outcome. When you are solving a problem using Six Sigma, you are getting a process to perform consistently, so the outcome is always successful.

A very simple example of this involved a problem at a medical-device manufacturer, where they made a sterile product that had to get sealed in a pouch. The pouch was put on a conveyor belt and then traveled through a heat sealer. Three things could affect the seal: the temperature of the sealer, the pressure the sealer put on the pouch, and the speed of the belt. Using a Six Sigma tool called *Design of Experiments,* we were able to determine the optimal setting for all three. From that day forward, all three settings were held constant, and we never had sealer problems again. Six Sigma is about getting to a practical solution, but it's also about developing a consistent process that creates a consistent result.

Six Sigma Training

There are a variety of ways to conduct Six Sigma training. I have seen Green Belt training delivered in anywhere from three to ten days. I have also seen Green Belt training conducted with a minimal exposure to statistics. Instead, the focus was to come up with a "graphical" solution to the problem, as in many cases, by simply graphing the data gathered, significant differences appear that point to a solution. The approach here can be referred to as taking a *practical problem,* making it a *graphical problem*, finding a *graphical solution,* and translating that into a *practical solution.*

Training for the alternate belt colors (not green or black) often involves anywhere from one to three days. Training is at a very high level and is intended to engage the people in problem-solving and process-improvement. My feeling is that these belts are less effective since there is often no senior Black Belt or Master Black Belt overseeing their work and making sure that they remain engaged.

Training for Master Black Belts, Black Belts, and Quality Leaders are identical and typically take anywhere from ten to twenty days to perform. The people you put in these roles should be your best and brightest. They have to be able to handle the complexity that statistical analysis can bring, but they also must have both the patience and perseverance to drive the changes that their project creates.

12

INFLUENCING LEADERS

Sometimes, senior leaders in a business will object to having someone from outside their organization conduct a Six Sigma project in their department. A skilled Master Black Belt knows to address this early in the process by engaging that leader and explaining that this is a team effort to drive improvement. The Master Black Belt knows that the resistant leader must be in agreement, or the project will never succeed. Some leaders will fight you even if you are trying to help and are willing to share the credit. You need to have strong influencing skills to persuade these types of leaders. Just because you attended a meeting with their boss, who was in favor of the project, does not mean you will always get cooperation. Some leaders will support one position in a meeting with senior managers in the room but will secretly work against the process since they are concerned that the project could reveal their shortcomings as a leader.

The Stakeholder Analysis

For a project to be successful, you need to identify all your stakeholders and rank them as being strongly opposed, opposed, neutral, supportive, or strongly supportive. Next you must determine which of those stakeholders you need to move to a more favorable place on that continuum. But you have to build active relationships with all the key players to ensure that you are properly interpreting where they stand. Getting key opposed stakeholders to move to a supportive position is a huge win. It's also a critical element of any project and cannot be ignored. But do not share this Stakeholder Analysis beyond your small team. Doing so can have negative repercussions. A person may be opposed to the project, but they will likely not want that information available for others to see.

I have seen situations when projects were kicked off to help a business improve in an area where the overall leader knew there was an opportunity to drive an improvement, but that overall leader shut the project down. The overall leader was listening to his direct reports who were concerned about what the project might reveal. Had a relationship been built with the overall leader early in the process, that situation could have been avoided.

13

THE SIX SIGMA PROCESS

Finally, I want to walk through the two approaches for Six Sigma. This is intended to be a high-level overview. The first and most common is the DMAIC approach. This acronym stands for the five phases of the project: Define, Measure, Analyze, Improve, and Control. This approach is probably used in 95 percent of all projects across all businesses. I am going to focus on this approach and will provide a very brief description of the other approach at the end of the chapter.

Define

The Define phase is just as it is named. It's the phase where you define the problem and pull together a small team to help you drive your project from start to finish. Typically, feedback is gathered from customers (internal or external) of the process, and a project charter is completed. The charter involves defining the problem as it exists today, clarifying the scope of the project, listing the team members, and laying out a timeline to complete the five phases. Then a high-level process map is created for the process that you want to fix. A great tool for this is called either a SIPOC or COPIS—it depends on whether you want to list the customer first. It stands for Suppliers, Inputs, Process, Outputs, and Customers. The P stands for a high-level Process Map. For any process, you should be able to list the suppliers, inputs, outputs, and customers. Understanding all these elements helps you select the right team to evaluate the process.

That covers most of what you do in the Define phase. Never underestimate this phase. You need to make sure you have good feedback from your customers and can clearly articulate the problem they are experiencing. And again, customers can be internal or external to the business.

Measure

In the Measure phase, you perform three primary tasks. First, you list the factors that the customer views as being very important to them. Then you identify different metrics that you can track and see how they align with those factors that are very important to the customers. Typically one of the metrics will stand out as being the one that, if improved, will have the biggest effect on the most important factors to the customer. A great example around selecting a metric involved a business in India that provided transportation for many of its workers to get to the office. They had a fleet of vehicles from sixty-person buses to twenty-five-person shuttles, to twelve-person vans to five-person cars. These vehicles would pick people up at key points in the city and bring them to the office. Over time the transportation costs became very high. When a table was built comparing the possible metrics to the factors important to the customer, the metric that emerged was "Empty Seats Per Day." Drivers counted the number of empty seats they had on each return run, helping them recognize where the issues were.

Next you collect your data around that metric and then go through a process to make sure the data is valid. By *valid,* I mean that it is correct and entered correctly into a business system. This is really important. I can think of a number of times where people have come to me with data, a list of client information, for example, and said that the data must be valid because it came right out of the business's system. I always send them back and tell them to find the source of the data— ideally tracking it back to a document the customer filled out. That original document is the *truth,* since it reflects exactly what the customer wanted. In many cases, the Green Belts and Black Belts found errors in the business systems. I cannot stress the importance of ensuring your data is valid. This goes beyond Six Sigma, in any job you do, if you are gathering data, you need to have valid data.

Not only does the data need to be valid, but it cannot have a bias, or be too reflective of a special group of customers. A great example involves a magazine called *Literary Digest.* It had a circulation of around one million households in 1936. It had successfully predicted the winner of the US Presidential elections in 1916, 1920, 1924, 1928, and 1932. It was poised to achieve the same success in 1936, but sought to grow the population of those surveyed, and was able to poll nearly 10 million households through buying lists of people who had telephones or owned cars. The response rate was in the mid-20 percent range, and the results were published in the October 31 issue, indicating that the Republican candidate, Alf Landon would defeat the Democratic incumbent Franklin Roosevelt in the November election. At the same time, a young man who surveyed a mere 50,000 people using a better sampling process stated that Roosevelt would win the election. Needless to say, we know the outcome—the *Literary Digest* was wrong. Why? Because their survey data had a strong bias toward the wealthier members of Depression-era America. They had polled people who owned telephones and automobiles, and in 1936, people who owned telephones and automobiles tended to be wealthier than the average American. Wealthier Americans tended to vote for Republican candidates. Interestingly, the young man who accurately predicted Roosevelt's reelection went on to become a household name: George Gallup. The key takeaway here is to make sure that the data you are collecting does not have any bias.

Once the data has been determined to be correct, the project moves into the Analyze phase.

Analyze

In the Analyze phase you collect data on the factors that might influence your metrics. So let's return to the example of improving the quarterly-volume-per-rep metric. Data was collected around:

- How many years the reps had worked in sales
- How many years they had worked in sales at the current company
- How large their territory was geographically
- How large their territory was in terms of population
- Their level of education
- How long they had been in their territory
- How many miles they put on their company car
- Whether they had ever worked in an underwriting group that evaluated and approved each financing deal
- The number of target companies estimated to be in their territory.

To identify these factors, brainstorm. Assemble a cross-functional group of people involved in the process, asking them to come up with ideas of factors that could influence the metric. Asking people to think of factors that fall within the following six categories beginning with the letter "M" can be helpful: man, method, material, machine, measurement, and Mother Nature. For example, under measurement you would list the how measurements in the process can affect your metric, such as a scale that is not calibrated. Or under Mother Nature you would list environmental factors that can affect the metric, such as delays caused by a month-end closing process. It will depend on what your metric is and what factors can affect that metric. The tool used to organize the ideas collected in these categories is called the Cause and Effect Diagram. It's also referred to as a Fishbone. The causes appear in the bones of the fish, and the effect goes at the head of the fish. Please see the image below.

Cause and Effect Diagram (Fishbone)

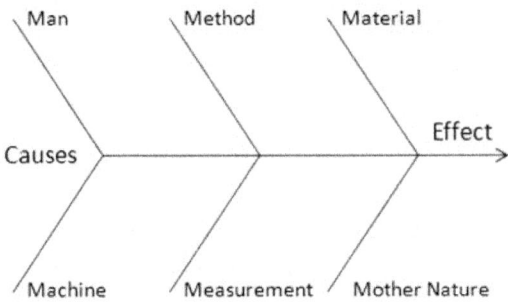

Once you have all this data, you need to perform two tasks before beginning your analysis of the data.

First, determine how you are performing against your metric. Look at what the metric is telling you. To use the earlier example of improving the sales rep volume, if we plotted the data and saw that the average volume was $30 million per year, that is how the sales reps are performing.

Second, determine the desired level of improvement. We may want to get that up from $30 million to an average of $33 million per rep. Or we may want to focus on bringing up the lower performers. There are several ways to look at it. The person leading the project needs to discuss the options with the stakeholders, but the right improvement target has to be identified as the second task.

Finally, begin the analysis of the data. Study every factor to determine which one or ones are influencing the performance of the overall metric. This is where most of the statistical testing takes place, as each factor is studied to determine if it is influencing the outcome.

Improve

In the Improve phase, you'll summarize the analyzed data, and present the vital factors you have identified. In some cases, when you have multiple factors that are significant, you may need the help of a seasoned Master Black Belt to determine which factor is really the one influencing the results. Once that critical factor is identified, conduct a pilot to confirm that the correlation found does in fact cause the poorer performance. The phrase "*correlation* does not mean *causation*" is critical to anyone who is studying correlations, just as we covered earlier in this book.

It's very important that the pilot be run on only a portion of the process, so you can compare the effect of the change against the existing process in the same timeframe. People often believe that after making a change to the entire process, their new statistical data can be compared against the company's former numbers. But what if something else happened to change after you rolled out your change, and the other change caused an improved performance across the board? How do you know which one is really driving the change? Always try to pilot your solution with a subset of the overall group so you can see that the subset that did not get the change continued to perform as expected.

Measurement error can also impact your process. In some projects, you may be able to determine that if your critical factor is within a certain range, your metric will always be in an acceptable range. You have to ensure that you can measure the factor precisely and accurately. If there is a possibility of measurement error, you may have to tighten the acceptable range for the factor, which will in turn tighten the acceptable range for the metric. But it will ensure your process does not produce defects created by measurement error.

Control

In the Control phase, there are three important tasks. First, now that you know what your critical factor is, you may need to verify that your source for that data point is always correct. To paraphrase, just as you confirmed your data source for your metric was valid, you have to do that for the factor you found to be influencing the metric.

The second step is to review the results of your pilot and confirm that by adjusting the significant factor, you saw an improvement in your metric. At this point, you either achieved your desired improvement or not. If you did not, you should go back in the process to an earlier phase and restart at that point. How far back should you go? It depends on what your results are telling or not telling you. In extreme cases, you may have chosen the wrong metric and need to go back to Measure. Or perhaps you did not consider enough influencing factors, and have to go back to the Analyze phase and analyze a few more factors. Or perhaps an error existed in how your pilot was conducted; then you should return to the Improve phase. In most cases, if you followed the DMIAC process properly, you will not have to worry about the results, since you will likely achieve what you set out to accomplish. But you are not done.

Once you have conducted all this work, you must put a control plan in place. This is critical. You should identify a way to control the factor that makes the process perform better, so that it will not slip back to its old setting, causing you to lose all that you have gained. Make sure you put time into this last part of the process, or all your work is for nothing.

That covers the DMAIC approach from a high level. There are many tools that can be used along the way, but I've chosen not to delve into that level of detail, as this book is intended to give you a high-level view of the benefits of Six Sigma, as well as several other strategies for improving a business.

The other Six Sigma methodology is referred to as DMADV or DFSS. DMADV stands for Define, Measure, Analyze, Design, and Verify. It has evolved into DMADOV, where the O stands for Optimize, and it forms the basis for the DFSS, or the Design For Six Sigma methodology. In simple terms, all three are virtually the same. They are used when you do not have a process or a product today, and you want to create one. The methodology provides a format with milestone reviews that includes multiple tools to determine what is the optimal approach. Many of GE's businesses credit the DFSS approach with allowing them to design and build better products with a slightly higher early-development stage cost, but a substantially lower later-development stage cost, as most of the design bugs are determined early on and avoided. This allows a product to be delivered to market much faster, providing a nice competitive advantage.

14

A FEW FINAL POINTS ON SIX SIGMA

Aspects of any business that provide a natural feed into a Six Sigma program are the customer-complaints or product-returns groups. In manufacturing, when a product is returned for a quality issue (which could include an order entry error that shipped them the wrong product), that product should have a report summarizing the customer's complaint and the surrounding information. For each of these returns, a team should sit down and review how to handle the situation. This may involve sending product to a design engineer to evaluate, or to a manufacturing engineer to review how it was processed. In every case, after the returned product was analyzed, the returned product should be classified into one of the following four categories: Design Problem, Processing Problem, Purchased Component Problem, or Unable to Determine. A good team will minimize the number that fall in the final category.

This team should be comprised of the heads of Manufacturing, Manufacturing Engineering, Engineering, and

Quality Control. They should meet every week to keep the process moving, providing prompt feedback to customers. For service companies, which include financial service companies, this process may require a centralized system that allows multiple functions to input complaints, since many people across the business come in regular contact with the customer. Here again, a team of key leaders needs to be assembled to evaluate every problem. Once evaluated, the problem is placed into a root-cause category: an Inherent Flaw in the Service, an Internal-Process Issue, a Customer-Communication issue, a Supplier-Created Issue, or Unable to Determine. The final category should only be used as a last resort.

World-class businesses conduct this level of analysis on their business, as they know this form of customer feedback is critical to their success. Failure to provide a high-quality product or service (or to fail to catch the deterioration of the product or service's quality) can be fatal to a business.

Let me finish the Six Sigma section with a surprising discovery. A division of GE had nearly a hundred Black Belts focused on improving customer delivery times. After nearly a year of work, they reported to management that they had improved the delivery performance numbers. But surveys of the customers continued to show the same level of dissatisfaction. In analyzing the process further, it was discovered that the Black Belts had reduced the *average* number of days late on all shipments. But when GE looked at the *variation* around the performance, both before and after the changes, the numbers did not change. In other words, the customer was "feeling" the variation—one order shipped on time, the next sixteen days late, the next five days late, the next three days early. The customer wanted the delivery on the requested day, but based on those actual delivery numbers, they had no idea when it would come. Improving the average benefitted GE, as they were able to collect payment for product shipped sooner, but it provided no perceived benefit to the customer.

Upon realizing this, the company redefined how it looked at customer deliveries and started looking at a metric called Span. Span was calculated by looking at the prior month's shipments and looking at the variation from delivery date. With all the data plotted, they took the number of days where only five percent of all that month's shipments were earlier, and then took the number of days where only five percent of the shipments were later, and then took the difference of those two numbers. That number was the *Span*. The goal is to get that number to be as small as possible and then start tracking the difference between the numbers where only one percent of the month's shipments are earlier and one percent are later. Take a look at the plot on the next page. It provides an example of a company's shipments in one month.

This method can be useful if the business involved is large and many factors are contributing to missing customer-delivery dates. Interestingly, getting the business to think about measuring the customer performance around variation and not around average was such an important issue to GE that Jack Welch included it in his letter to the shareholders in the *1998 GE Annual Report*.

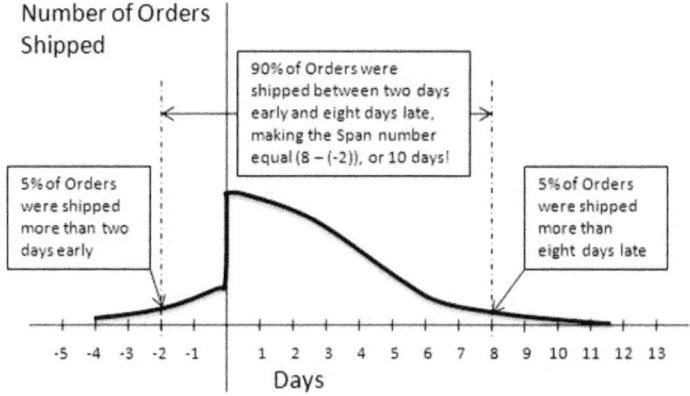

Number of Orders Shipped

90% of Orders were shipped between two days early and eight days late, making the Span number equal (8 − (-2)), or 10 days!

5% of Orders were shipped more than two days early

5% of Orders were shipped more than eight days late

-5 -4 -3 -2 -1   1 2 3 4 5 6 7 8 9 10 11 12 13

Days

In the Turnaround section, I describe a business where we improved our on-time delivery from 53 percent to over 99 percent just by having a cross-functional team dive into the problem. Some businesses today use a concept called Perfect Order Reliability. It is the product of four different percentages: percent complete, percent on-time, percent damage-free, and percent with appropriate paperwork. Multiplying all four percents together produces the Perfect Order Reliability percentage. You have to decide what approach and level of analytics works best for your business.

Part IV

People and Change

15

MANAGING HEADCOUNT

Again, for a business to be competitive, it needs to employ the right number of people. This section provides ideas on how to identify where there may be opportunities to improve staffing levels.

Consider how a business evolves over time. When the business is growing and it encounters problems, people are hired to help out. When a recession occurs, the marketplace contracts; businesses respond by reducing their costs to remain competitive. Those cost cuts often include layoffs.

Consider what was going on in those businesses before the recessionary or declining revenue period arrived. People had been hired into businesses to perform jobs that may have been new to the business. In most cases, the newly hired people determined the most-efficient way to do the job, often creating less work for them to perform. Some might have asked for more work, but many probably didn't. So over time, businesses—especially larger businesses—end up with excessive headcount. Businesses or departments that have cyclical workloads will frequently experience this. Now consider that many lower-level managers are often hesitant to reduce the size of their departments. They may choose to run the group with extra people in case they are told they need to let a few people go. Some people have no problem working in a job that has a very light workload, but carrying extra resources can significantly limit a business's ability to be competitive. It is often difficult to recognize whether this overstaffed situation exists unless you are familiar with the jobs in that department.

For larger corporations, hiring college graduates into rotational programs can provide a great perspective. They join the business with no preconceived notions and can offer an objective perspective about where excessive headcount exists as they rotate through different departments. In smaller businesses, this can only be accomplished by routinely walking around and observing employees' activity. Over time, it becomes easier to recognize who is busy and who is not.

Now let's return to a theme mentioned earlier in the book. Jobs will tend to migrate to the lower-cost markets. The only way to keep jobs in the United States is for businesses to be very competitive in their marketplace. Businesses that are overstaffed are carrying costs that make them less competitive. These businesses are at a greater risk of being underpriced and replaced by a competitor in a lower-cost labor market. But what if the business decides to stop hiring and lets natural attrition bring the headcount level down by reassigning people in the overstaffed areas to replace the people that leave for retirement or a better opportunity. This is the approach many businesses need to take, because if they do not remain competitive, all their jobs will be lost to a lower-cost labor market. From my observations over more than twenty-five years—and they are reconfirmed on almost a weekly basis— virtually any business can cut 20 percent of its workforce and still meet its numbers.

By lower-cost labor markets, I'm referring to emerging-market countries that pay employees anywhere from less than 10 percent up to 25 percent of what the same worker is paid in the United States. I have walked through government-owned factories in China, privately and publically traded companies in India, and even Maquiladoras in Mexico. I have seen similar or worse inefficiencies in the way some of those businesses operate. But given how low the wages are in all those markets, those businesses can afford to be very inefficient. We cannot. I'd much rather see a US-based business cut back its staffing by 20 percent through attrition and keep the other 80 percent of jobs here in the United States than see 100 percent of the jobs in the business move to another country.

So how does a business address this issue? I see two methods. One is an approach described earlier: Assign growth targets to businesses, forcing them not only to grow the top line, but also manage the bottom line. If they fail to hit their increased top-line numbers, the only other way to grow the bottom line is through reducing costs. This approach drives what I call *operating-manager behavior*, where the business must look inward to reduce costs to make its bottom line number. The other approach is to invest in training the middle managers to recognize these cost-reduction opportunities. Teaching them to walk through their departments, making observations, is valuable. Or they can spend a few days working in their employees' area.

A great story involves a very bright young manager who was working to improve the efficiency of her call center team. She chose to work in an unused cube in her team's area and observe. She also worked with IT to understand how often some of her employees were on the Internet. Analyzing her observations and the IT data, she discovered one individual through whom many questions were routed, who claimed to be too busy to do anything beyond his current responsibilities. Research showed that he was not even 50-percent efficient. More than 50 percent of his time was being spent on non-work-related activity. Because he handled a lot of small tasks, he appeared to be very busy. Perception and reality can often be two very different things. This young manager ultimately changed the workflow in the group, reducing staffing needs by 20 percent by better utilizing those that remained.

I have always been a big fan of strictly limiting hiring or instituting a hiring freeze and having managers work together to share resources. Managers who do not want their people helping other groups, though these people are not busy all day long, should be replaced. When I was a front-line manager, I always emphasized the need to work together. I once had a team of talented test engineers who designed and built test equipment for the production floor. They had a host of responsibilities. Every quarter, I updated their project lists and reminded them that if one of them failed in completing his assignments on time, they all failed. They were in this together, and even though they may not have liked each other, they pitched in and always helped each other out. They always hit their deadlines because they worked as a team.

I'm not advocating that every US business cut its workforce by 20 percent, but I'm appealing to every manager reading this book to understand that it is better for the US economy to keep four jobs locally than send five overseas. If we do not perform our work efficiently here, someone can easily afford to do it less efficiently elsewhere in a lower-cost labor market. Not replacing people when they leave or change jobs in the company is the best way to reduce headcount.

I have one more statistic that is worth noting: In the major turnarounds I was involved in, we cut the workforce in half and produced either the same or more products and services than we had been producing before. Those situations were driven by a crisis, and were easier to justify. But why wait for a crisis situation that the business may not recover from, when changes can be made today to increase the likelihood of avoiding the crisis?

Any company going through a turnaround needs to handle the situation of reducing headcount in a very professional manner. When we converted a medical-device factory to Lean, we had thirty roaming shop-floor inspectors who had a very negative effect on morale. They were great people, but the process of approaching assemblers and telling them they are making mistakes can create an adversarial relationship. Quality has to be built into a product, not inspected into it. We knew these roaming floor-inspector roles were going to be eliminated, so rather than spring layoff notices on them when the day came, we notified them very early in the turnaround process that in one year, none of their jobs would be there. We explained to them that this would allow them time to find a different role in the company, or if they really wanted to continue doing what they were doing, they could seek employment elsewhere. Some stayed and some left, but the right message was sent to every employee in the company.

16

TRAINING

I've often heard senior leaders criticize the idea of training. Some training, I agree, can be a waste of time. But I will walk through a few examples of how training can be very beneficial.

Many people are aware of large Fortune 100 companies having large training centers with a dedicated campus. Extensive training programs are offered, including Ivy League professors as instructors. This kind of training can be extremely valuable for several reasons. Most importantly, it is an investment in human capital. People represent a major expenditure in most businesses, so investing in improving their performance is critical. Second, these training classes can be morale boosters, and if the classes are structured properly, they can really develop the students to think more broadly and make better decisions. I witnessed this firsthand. I was nominated to attend a three-week training course at GE's Crotonville training center. It provided a great opportunity to learn and network with a talented group of GE leaders.

Training Shop-Floor Workers to Learn New Skills

Another great story around training that is attributed to W. Edwards Deming. He observed that training in the United States was conducted in the following fashion. Let's say that Al is doing a job. He gets promoted and trains Bill. Bill gets a new opportunity and trains Carl. Carl is soon moved to another department and trains Dave. Dave decides to retire, but before going, trains Ed. Finally, Ed moves to a better job and trains Frank. So Al started everything off by training Bill, who trained Carl, who trained Dave, who trained Ed, who trained Frank. Keep that chain of training in mind while we consider the process in Japan.

In Japan, a worker being moved to a different job is sent to the training department and trained using a documented process, and after three to four weeks, she is now able to do the job. When comparing the two approaches, the Japanese approach suggests a more consistent approach, since every worker is put through the same training process. The US approach is like the Telephone Game, where one person tells a story to the next, who tells the next person, who tells the next, and so on. In our example, the job Al was doing is most likely different from the job that Frank ends up doing, since many issues get lost or reemphasized as each operator puts his own spin on how things should be done. It is in our US culture to be individuals, whose ideas influence actions, therefore causing a different approach to be taken when several people tackle the same job. A good training program can help address this issue. Identifying the best possible way to perform a task and training everyone to perform it the same way helps drive a consistent performance throughout the company that the customer expects. Even if the best process is identified and implemented, it should still be reviewed periodically to make sure it is still the best practice.

While the previous story emphasizes the value of a consistent training program, training can be used to advance workers into better-paying jobs, and cross-training can be used to significantly strengthen the workforce and reduce operating costs in any business.

In any business with a skilled factory worker or office worker, an opportunity to establish a training program exists. The training program can be set up to train people to learn the skills of higher-level jobs in the organization. When those jobs open up, the candidates who have completed their training can be considered qualified candidates for those roles. We set this up in one of our manufacturing facilities, and many of the workers were very happy with the opportunities it created.

Let me explain: If work in an area slowed down, many of the workers would get trained to build that next level of skills. When that next-level job became available, that worker was already trained and qualified to take the job. This approach also allowed the business to maintain its required training records for its ISO 9001 certification (an internationally recognized quality-systems certification for manufacturers and service businesses).

Another purpose of training is to optimize the performance of the workforce. This training approach can be applied in a variety of settings—on factory floors, in back offices, or virtually anywhere. Many businesses with over a hundred floor workers, or a hundred people in the back office, can see significant improvements in productivity through cross-training.

Identify jobs with similar levels of difficulty and group them together. Ideally, target areas that might be counter-cyclical, so that when one area is slow, the workers can be reassigned to the area that is busier. The best approach is to lump jobs together in groups of six. The average wage for workers in any group should be equal to having mastered three to four of the six possible jobs in that group. When new employees are hired, they come in at a base rate that goes up with each new job they master. Existing employees get $500- or $1,000-dollar bonuses for each job they master until they acquire a job in the group that raises their pay above its current level. At that point, they no longer get the bonus, but their wage rate is rises to the rate that is associated with mastering each additional job.

Think about the benefits this creates for everyone. It gives a financial incentive to employees to improve their skills. It also builds a more flexible workforce for the business. And it can also provide the company with a different way of retaining employees in the event of a reduction in force. Rather than using seniority to determine who to keep and who to let go, a company can use the employees' skill levels instead, keeping those that have all six jobs mastered first, then those with five, and so on.

Clearly for this process to be effective, the training and certification process for each job needs to be well documented. Those employees that have multiple skills should cycle through the different jobs on a regular basis to keep their knowledge of each job fresh.

17

MANAGING PEOPLE THROUGH CHANGE

In the late 1980s, I was involved with a company wrestling with whether or not to establish a second manufacturing site in the South. A very bright vice president of operations argued that while the business was booming, it did not make sense to generate the additional overhead of two manufacturing sites. He argued that the company should wait until the Northern plant hit capacity before initiating any expansion. While his logic was sound, his recommendation was not delivered in a one-on-one setting, but in front of a larger group. He received a strong berating from the group vice president, a manager two levels above him, and later, he saw his career progression come to an end. In less than two years, he was no longer with the company. Ultimately, the business did not move, but reinvested in the Northern site to increase its capacity. But presenting a very logical rebuttal in the wrong setting had been a grave political mistake for the vice president of operations. Some managers are open to discussing different perspectives in a group setting, but others are not. Building relationships with your senior leaders can help you understand how they operate.

The biggest challenge in every case is engaging people in driving change. The resistance to change can rise to fairly high levels in the organization, creating the most difficult situation of all. I recently spoke with a consultant hired to drive improvements in a business. In the initial report to the client, the consultant identified a senior leader as someone who needed to change or be replaced if the business was to move forward in the right direction.

What happened next? That problematic person was promoted, became the consultant's primary contact, and read the entire report. Imagine how that person reacted!

If you were presented with this situation, what would you do? My recommendation would be to sit down with both the problematic new contact and the leader who promoted him. Then I'd lay out the go-forward plan and tactfully encourage the two to either move forward with the plan, or discontinue the consulting arrangement. One other takeaway is that criticism of employees is best delivered verbally.

A detailed and energetic CEO I know was faced with a challenge. One of his senior leaders tended to engage in activities considered inappropriate with customers, and the CEO was concerned that it could create a compromising position for the business since it was not clear if this person was acting objectively and conducting business in a professional manner. When he pursued this person's termination with the board, he found himself without a job. This person apparently had a connection with a senior member of the board and used that influence to keep his job. Any leader seeking to take action on an employee needs to test the water first. Work with the Human Resources team, and run it by a few trusted confidants on the board.

Another interesting case involved a talented senior packaging engineer who ran the packaging department at a well-known pen manufacturer. Marketing had decided to run a promotion putting thirteen pens in a twelve-pen box. When this was presented to the senior packaging engineer, he said that he would determine if this was possible. Before conducting any tests, the senior packaging engineer ran it by his boss, the vice president of operations. His boss became enraged, saying the idea was ridiculous and was an unnecessary giveaway that would not work. He told the senior packaging engineer to go back and tell Marketing that it would not work. He did so in a meeting that included an owner of the company. Twelve months later, Marketing came back with the same request, and he ran it by his boss again, and once again, his boss told him in a rage to explain to Marketing that it could not be done. The engineer delivered the message again.

But the senior packaging engineer was curious. So, one night on the second shift, he worked with the second-shift foreman to see if it was possible. Sure enough, it worked.

Several months later, the vice president of operations who had opposed the thirteen-pen promotion was let go for other reasons, and the second-shift foreman was promoted to vice president of operations. Marketing was still eager to run the thirteen-pen promotion and asked the newly promoted vice president of operations if they could put thirteen pens in a twelve-pen box. His response was that they could do it, and he knew it was possible because he had witnessed the senior packaging engineer do it on the second shift. Needless to say, the owner called the senior packaging engineer into his office and terminated him, telling him that he could no longer trust what he said. Had the senior packaging engineer not conducted the trials to put thirteen pens in a twelve-pen box, he could have easily explained that his boss had refused to let him explore the option and, thus, saved his own job.

What is the common thread between these anecdotes? While every one of these people were bright and talented contributors, they were all trying to do the "right thing," and ended up losing their job or their client. And in most cases, the same results could have been achieved without the costly results. Obviously, it is easy to be a Monday-morning-quarterback, but these are great lessons for anyone who wants to drive change. It is not just about the process change; it is more about the people. This book is about driving change in a business, and to be successful, you need to engage the right people at the right time in the right setting.

In the Six Sigma section of this book, the Stakeholder Analysis is described, where one reviews whether someone is strongly opposed, opposed, neutral, supportive, or strongly supportive to a proposed change. Every name evaluated on that page is a key player in the process change. Not every situation requires this level of analysis, but we need to recognize that when we drive change, more important than any process or product change is the fact we are asking people to change. Some can, and some cannot. By properly identifying and engaging the right people early in the process and keeping them informed throughout the process, we not only build credibility with key people in the business, but we avoid getting derailed by a leader with a separate and perhaps hidden agenda. I cannot emphasize the value of the Stakeholder Analysis enough—but you cannot share that Stakeholder Analysis beyond your small team of change agents. It contains sensitive information that could cause negative reactions. Use it wisely.

One more important anecdote: Several years ago, there was a great medical article that appeared on the web about patients with heart disease whose doctors ordered them to change their dietary and exercise habits. Two years later, the patients were interviewed to determine whether or not they were still following the dietary and exercise regimen. Keep in mind that these patients were faced with death if they did not change their habits. What percentage do you think was still following the doctors' orders? *Ten percent.*

Obviously, the change in diet and addition of exercise were not things these people wanted to do, even in the face of death. But dietary changes and increased exercise are often perceived as unpleasant and more work. Keep this in mind when you are changing behavior in your businesses. While resistance should be expected, if the new process is simpler and easier to apply, we will find it much easier to get nearly everyone to embrace the change. Encourage your change agents to strive for simplicity in their solutions.

I'm going to reemphasize an earlier point that ties in with getting people to change. In a major turnaround, where the business needs to change how it is operating, a new set of leaders is often required. This is usually required because the current set of leaders likely created the problems that the business is now in. When I've found myself in turnaround situations, I've typically seen between 80 percent and 90 percent of the leadership team turn over. The changes cannot stop with the leadership team. In large companies, that change may need to go several layers deep. Getting the right people in the right jobs is critical to driving a successful turnaround in the long run.

Part V

Other Points to Consider

18

TURNAROUNDS

The word *turnaround* often makes people think of a crisis situation when a business is virtually out of cash and about to become bankrupt. People whose entire career is dedicated to helping those businesses restore profitability recognize how to identify product lines or entire businesses that should be sold off or shut down. At the same time, they streamline the core business process and reduce the time to collect money from customers, while deferring payments to help increase cash on hand. These turnaround managers will build thirteen-week cash-flow models to have adequate cash on hand to keep the business running. These *turnaround managers* can often move on to the next troubled business once the business has stabilized. The leadership team will typically be replaced, and depending on the size of the business, many middle-level managers may have to be replaced, too. These changes require a different approach and mindset to restore the desired levels of profitability.

While the above is an extreme case, there are businesses that are operating with positive cash flow but are not optimizing the business to maximize profitability and efficiency. Think about it from an employee's perspective. Everyone would like to see the hassles removed from their jobs. For example, a simple request may require five signatures and takes several days. But many businesses and people will tolerate these hassles, accepting that this is how they operate. Realistically, that business could be an excellent candidate for a turnaround. Getting the right objective person in to evaluate the business could prove to be a great investment.

Financial Services Turnarounds

Remember the financial services turnaround I discussed earlier? New-deal volume had disappeared when the business was put inside of a large business with a different set of investment approvers. The new investment approvers would not approve the loans and leases that ultimately depended on another round of equity funding to repay the loan. To turn this business around, we started by analyzing the company's investment history. We determined the underwriting criteria that was common to loans and leases that had the highest frequency of paying back in full. Once that data was presented to the investment approvers, they agreed to resume funding the loans and leases that met the new investment criteria.

Manufacturing Turnarounds

The high-voltage wire-and-cable business I referred to earlier went through some very tough times as well. During the housing boom of the late 1980s, utilities were buying underground residential-distribution cable at a very rapid pace. The US economy saw the increased purchase of homes driven by the Baby Boomers coming of age and buying homes. Real Estate prices moved up rapidly. In a three-year period, some buyers saw a nearly doubling of their home values in some areas. The demand for homes meant an increase in new homes being built, leading to a demand for underground residential-distribution cable. So this business saw demand for its products take off in the late 1980s. These businesses responded to the demand for product by adding capacity. When the recession hit in 1990, it slowed home purchases and home building significantly, thus creating an over capacity on the supply side for the underground residential-distribution cable. When purchasing wire and cable, the utilities discovered that they could play the manufacturers against each other on price. Soon, the per-foot price of cable dropped by 30 percent or more in many cases.

We had a new general manager who had a wealth of experience in manufacturing. He had joined the parent company five years earlier and was brought in to run a different business that had been struggling. This business made a variety of products including surge arrestors and insulators used by utilities to avoid overloads and support power lines. On his first day, the group vice president pulled the new general manager aside and told him the business was for sale, and they were hoping to sell it soon. His response was simple. "If I can turn this business around, will you keep it?" He was told yes, so he began analyzing the business to improve its performance.

At the top of a utility pole, you often see bare wires, separated from the poles by insulators. Up through the 1980s, those insulators were ceramic. This business developed a much less-expensive, polymer-based insulator. The business faced several challenges, including ineffective leadership, overstaffing, and production issues with the polymer used in the insulators. Addressing the issues with leadership and the polymer-based insulator became two top priorities. The General Manager replaced several members of the leadership team and engaged the right people to work on the polymer-molding problem. Within a short time, the business had a 30-percent operating margin and dominated the market space in which it operated. The General Manager was reassigned to run the wire-and-cable business as well.

At its peak, the wire-and-cable business employed over 400 people, and over the years that followed, headcount dropped to just over 200. But amazingly, nearly the same volume of product was shipping every month. The business became very creative in accomplishing the same amount of work with fewer people. Every product line was analyzed, and the barely profitable product lines were eliminated, equipment was sold, and employees were reassigned or laid off. Every process in the business was scrutinized for efficiency, including the office administration. In one group, we had six people pricing requests for quotes on cables. When it was discovered that the computer systems could produce the same quotes within a few percent of the pricing team's calculation, the group was disbanded, but one person was kept in place to price the more-complex quotes. Nearly every department decreased in size by one-third, and some by 50 percent or more. Everyone remaining was assigned additional work.

Much of the quality assurance work was automated, and the repeated inspection and measurement of product was eliminated. The automated Quality Assurance System allowed the extruder operators to enter their measured wall thicknesses that were then visually checked at final test, eliminating three or four unnecessary re-inspections. That same system allowed for the collection and storage of all the important QA data. It replaced a manual process that had involved going through sheets of data to create a report in the form of a certification sent to a customer. Soon that process was fully automated, and with a few clicks of a button, the data was automatically retrieved and could be printed, signed, and shipped to the customer. It took over a year to introduce all these changes, but they improved the cost structure of the business.

Other areas targeted to reduce unnecessary expenses included workman's compensation, totaling over $1 million in expenses every year. In the area of worker's compensation, the company was averaging nearly one lost-time accident per week. This extraordinary high number had to be addressed. The business had developed a culture where accidents were expected to happen on a routine basis, and that had to change. Going forward, every department had to begin its shift or day with a brief meeting. That meeting had to include a discussion about safety. Every accident was investigated, and corrective and preventive changes were put in place. Every inconsistency in the events surrounding the accident was scrutinized. Within one year, the workman's compensation number dropped to less than $30,000, and there was only one lost-time accident that year. Much of the problem was discovered to have been attitude based. Employees had not taken safety seriously enough.

When all these changes were in place, the business ran with half the headcount and still shipped the same amount of product every month. Over 80 percent of the leadership team had been replaced with new leaders who brought a different perspective. This turnaround followed a common formula: change leadership, eliminate unprofitable products, minimize non-value-added activity, and streamline processes. Automated solutions were introduced wherever possible. The business went from a pre-recession 20-percent-plus operating-margin business to a 6-percent-operating-margin business, but it survived.

Another turnaround example involves a manufacturer of medical electronics and sterile disposable devices. It had recently changed hands. The new owners began replacing the leadership team, starting at the top. This business was generating about $60 million in sales, but it carried $24 million in inventory and was shipping only 53 percent of its products to its customers on time. It was losing market share and needed help. This turnaround began by having meetings with the employees to introduce the new leaders and to gather their thoughts.

In these meetings, when the subject of implementing Lean came up, there was a consistent response of, "Don't waste your time; we tried that here, and it does not work." In the past, a prominent accounting firm had sent in some consultants who had introduced managers and the employees to Lean. They had showed them how it worked and had told them to do it, but that is where the process had broken down. The employees had no motivation to go implement a system that a group of consultants had thrust upon them, telling them they had to do it. So this just added to our challenge of introducing Lean. This business needed more than just Lean— it needed a complete turnaround.

First, the unprofitable product lines were quickly identified and eliminated, and the remaining inventory and equipment was sold. People in key leadership positions were replaced, and in some cases, so were the people in the entire department beneath them. Cross-functional, self-directed work teams were formed to address the issues of shifting to Lean, improving on-time delivery, and reducing inventory. The stockroom was overflowing with excess material that contributed to a large "excess and obsolete" inventory. Non-value-added activity was identified and eliminated.

When the conversion to Lean was completed, only half of the 178,000-square-foot factory was occupied. Furthermore, other factories were then consolidated into the building. The products produced using Lean had better quality, and through the work of the First-Pass Yield team, the first-pass yield on products rose from the high 40-percent range to the high 90-percent range, and 99 percent of orders shipped on time. Revenues grew from $60 million to $150 million, and the factory was only 80 percent filled. The significant cultural change this business experienced is covered later in this book.

These were just a few examples of how a turnaround typically unfolds. Costs must be reduced quickly, and unprofitable product lines have to go. Leadership teams have to change to bring in the right type of thinking. Streamlining processes, focusing on quality products, and meeting customer delivery requests are critical. Cash management can be critical as well. In extreme cases, increased pay-early discounts can be offered to bring cash in faster, and payables need to be deferred. Every turnaround has its unique challenges, but often a common formula with a few variations can be applied to fix a business.

19

COMMUNICATION STRATEGY

When driving meaningful change in a company, you need to spread your message throughout the business in as many ways as you can. A self-directed, cross-functional work team comprised of the business's informal leaders can be a very powerful way of announcing that change is on the way. As these prominent team members go back to their departments and share the ideas raised in the team meetings, new ideas are often created. The new ideas are brought back to the team meeting. This is a subtle, but powerful communication process that helps inspire a culture of change. But you'll need more than just these influencers to carry your message.

Introducing a morning meeting in every department every day is a great way to get the message out about change. Remember the business saddled with the $1 million worker's compensation costs and how a daily morning meeting was introduced to get people talking about safety issues? Those discussions were not just about safety; they also included updates on what was changing in the business, and how the business's backlog was faring. These daily meetings were only ten minutes long, but they helped kill the inaccurate rumor mill that seems to flourish when a business goes through a change. At these meetings, facts were provided, and employees genuinely appreciated the candor. These meetings were great because communication is critical to the success of a business. Once the business survived the crisis, senior management no longer mandated these meetings, but many managers continued to hold them, in some cases dropping the frequency to anywhere from one to three times a week.

Another effective communication technique is to conduct a monthly meeting with all employees in the business. Use this meeting to share how the business is performing financially, reinforce the company's vision and strategy, and provide updates on changes. At the end of the meeting, take questions. Every business should reach out to its employees on a quarterly basis, but businesses going through significant changes should target monthly meetings. Let your employees hear their senior leaders, and give them the opportunity to raise issues that they feel are important.

It is all about building relationships and trust. When you give your employees the facts about why you are making changes, they feel that you trust them. In return, most employees will trust you back—and support the changes. Granted, there are always those who resist change, but while they can be a burden in the change process, they can also be a great source of counterpoints and ideas that may not have been considered. Unless these resisters of change are generating great dissension in the ranks, they always should be included and heard. Often, if a malcontent disrupts an all-employee meeting unnecessarily, his coworkers will voice their disapproval, and the complainer will typically back down.

In one business, we had a three-shift operation, so we conducted four meetings each month to get the message out. We typically started at 5:00 a.m. or 7:00 a.m. with the first and third shifts, covered the first shift and the office at 7:00 a.m. or 9:00 a.m., more of the office and the first and second shift at 1:00 p.m., and then covered anyone else at 3:00 p.m. These were long days, but the meetings were always well received by most attendees.

Leaders cannot drive change by hiding in their offices. They need to be visible and vocal about what the business is going through. When employees become concerned about how the changes may affect them, the reaction of some is to find a job elsewhere, and often, the most-talented leave first. When senior leaders candidly address employee concerns, these people are more likely to feel important and included in the process, and are therefore more likely to stay.

20

CALL CENTERS

Call centers can be a great area to look for process improvements. Center leaders often tell me that they have many metrics allowing them to track performance, and that they know exactly how the call center is performing. The challenge to optimize call center staffing lies more in the way the processes are set up to support the call center. By establishing the optimal process within the call center, the call center can become much more productive. Below are three examples that elaborate on where opportunities for improvement may exist.

The productivity of call center teams are often determined by three factors: staffing levels, workflow, and subteam structure. When the latter two are not set up properly, the staffing levels will rise.

The first example concerns a center that took calls requiring an answer from someone else in the business and then followed up with the customer. The process was organized so that when the call center representative did not have an answer, all these inquiries were funneled through a single person in the call center, who routed them to the appropriate person for resolution. The person possessing the information had to provide the answer to the call center representative who had taken the call, and then the representative followed up with the customer. The intention was good: the process was designed to educate the call center representatives so that ideally, eventually, they would have the answer for the customer.

The problem was that the customers asked a wide variety of questions, and thus, a call center representative might go days, weeks, or months without having to answer a given question twice. This prevented the representatives from retaining the answers, and this, in turn, meant that the representatives had to keep calling the experts who *did* know the answers—hence the bottleneck. The solution was to have the person who knew the answer respond directly to the customer. It left the option open for the customer service representatives to follow up on their own for the answer, but it gave the customer the answer much faster—frequently in less than one day, which was the targeted performance level.

The second example, discussed earlier in the Six Sigma section, involves a business that created twelve teams and set the call router to send each client's call to the appropriate team. The center struggled to meet the goal of answering every call within sixty seconds. When the supervisor had the teams focus only on answering the calls, they were able to achieve it. Most calls resulted in work that had to be done after the call. If the call center representatives were required to answer the phones quickly, they did not have time to perform this after-call work. So either the customer reached a call center representative quickly and waited longer for a final response, or it took longer to answer the calls but the customer received a final response sooner. Either way, customer service was being impacted.

When the call patterns were studied, it became clear that there were too many teams with the same skills who were passing calls along to their colleagues only because the client calling in was not assigned to their team. Put simply, ten of the twelve teams did the same work, but each only took calls for its assigned clients. This is another example of how, when a process is not aligned to the workload, unnecessary constraints are created. Once those ten teams were merged, every representative could take every client's call. By eliminating the additional call rerouting, enough efficiency was gained to allow the entire call center to achieve the sixty-second goal and complete all the after-call work.

The third example involves a call center where the management team wanted to optimize the productivity of all the call center representatives. The challenge of any call center is managing the volatility of the call volume. When call volume is high, everyone is busy. When call volume is low, there can be many underutilized resources. But those periods of low call volume can represent an opportunity. Different work can be assigned to the call center representatives who are in periods of low call volume.

The challenge, however, is that every new call will interrupt progress towards completing this additional work. Most call routers are programmed to direct the call to the person who has had the longest period of inactivity. Thus, by the time a representative realizes that she has a moment to complete some of her non-call work, she is the most likely person to be routed a phone call.

But what if that could be changed so that a call center with ten active call-taking representatives, every hour, a different representative could take a turn being the primary target for incoming calls? If the first representative is busy, the call is routed to the second representative, and if the second representative is busy, it's routed to the third representative, and so on. Each hour the assignments could cycle, so that whoever was just the primary gets dropped to the last position, the second rotates to the primary, the third rotates to the second, etc. With this rotating approach, the bottom three representatives—those that are least likely to receive a call—can now be given other work to do, and their productivity will be much higher with a reduced level of calls. It proved to work well for the team since their efficiency went up, and it became very easy to track the calls to the lowest-priority call center representative each hour to see how many calls were handled, making it very easy to determine if an additional representative was needed in the call center.

The big takeaway here is to study the way the work flows through the call center. Frequently, process changes are made without the proper monitoring to understand how the customer is affected. Providing fast solutions to customer problems while minimizing the time required for after call work should be every call center's goal.

Part VI

Putting It All Together

21

FINAL THOUGHTS

The strategies in this book can help companies of any size understand how they can improve their bottom line, but I suspect that businesses with between $10 million and $500 million in revenue will see the biggest benefit. These may be stand-alone businesses, or subsidiaries in large corporations. The book is intended to provide a straightforward formula that is easily applied to any business.

Start by putting together a strategic planning process that engages the leadership team and the key people a level or two below them. This in turn allows for new ideas to be presented, but most importantly, when the entire leadership team and the key leaders below them are engaged in the plan, their level of commitment and ownership grows. It is a great way to reduce the unnecessary projects that lower-level leaders initiate because they do not understand the business's strategy and vision. Diverting resources to these activities is a drain on the business that impacts its ability to compete effectively.

The final Strategic Plan should identify three to five key initiatives on which the business will be focused in the coming year. Those activities may include top-line growth strategies including new product or service offerings, or initiatives focused on improving the performance of the sales force, optimizing the pricing strategy, or retaining more of the existing client base. Bottom-line strategies including streamlining the customer fulfillment process can also be targeted. The data within a business has been described as many companies' most under-utilized asset. Having an analyst or two who can focus on analyzing your business data is an investment with a great return to the business. In every business-improvement initiative, discoveries are made that often surprise people involved in the process.

Challenge the beliefs the business is built on to make sure they still are true today. Understand what is changing in your marketplace and how you are positioned to respond to, or better yet, to anticipate those changes.

I cannot emphasize enough the need to understand your business's people. Employees who may not be in senior roles can have significant influence on the business. An extreme case of this involved a factory worker engaged in a labor-intensive process. Once employees in this very large group (300+) hit a five-year anniversary, they were given shares in the privately held company. This astute worker went through the department and bought up those shares from workers who saw little value in them and were happy to turn them into cash. In 1969, when the company was acquired, the shares this worker accumulated made him one of the top shareholders in the parent company. He continued to work his old job, but did not hesitate to walk into the subsidiary company's president's office and express his concerns. Needless to say, the subsidiary president prudently listened to and addressed those concerns. But not every situation will be as easy to recognize as the example above, since people can drive hidden agendas under the business's radar. Meeting with key leaders and tactfully understanding the relationships that exist within a business and do not appear on an organizational chart, is important when driving change and anticipating where resistance may lie.

In any organization, certain people can be strong influencers and have the ear of senior leadership but are not easily identified as having that level of influence on the business. When you are working to change a company, you are really changing the behavior of the people in that company, and given that we are creatures of habit, this can be a tall undertaking. When driving those changes, make sure you understand where the roadblocks may appear. To be successful, you need to quickly recognize what products or services have to be discontinued and what changes must be made to those products and services that remain. Having a trusted confidant, someone who knows the players in the business and can provide objective guidance, is a very valuable resource. A person like that can help you recognize the dangers associated with those who may resist change.

My final suggestion is to listen. In every business I've ever worked with, the answer to the company's problems existed within that business already; it was just a question of whether or not the leadership team had allowed a culture to exist where ideas were allowed to rise to the top to be considered.

Back at the factory in Stamford, Connecticut, where I began my professional career, I was lucky enough to have a boss who threw challenges my way. As I successfully delivered on each challenge, the challenges grew larger. When I had two years under my belt, we had a process that involved vacuum casting a tungsten part in copper that seemed to be creating defects in the final product. The yield on the final product had dropped to less than 20 percent acceptable. Without this product, the early-warning missile detection systems up and down the East and West Coasts of North America would stop functioning. Since the customer was the US Government, a real concern existed that the government could order the factory to shut down all other production and only make these special power tubes. When multiple efforts failed to resolve the problem, I was asked by my manager to lead a cross-functional team that would solve the problem.

Sure enough, the answer to the problem existed within the business. The manufacturing of this item was overseen by a senior engineer with nearly forty years of experience who had corrected a different production problem with the tungsten part by adding a processing step. This new step initially caused no problems, but rather than cleaning the tungsten part, as it was intended, it was actually introducing contaminants. When I investigated the problem, my lack of experience proved to be a tremendous benefit. With no preconceived notions, I asked every question I could of everyone who might have an idea. A seasoned metallurgist who worked in a separate building had the answer, and he had already told the senior engineer. The senior engineer had dismissed the recommendation as nonsense, since the problem had showed up well after he'd made the processing change.

My cross-functional, self-directed work team recommended to the company president that we try a dual-processing approach for the next batch of tungsten parts. Half were processed the senior engineer's way; half were processed the way the metallurgist recommended. Several days later, we had a very poor yield on the senior engineer's parts, and the metallurgist's approach had created parts that were 100 percent acceptable. Problem solved.

The solutions to your business's problems already lie within the business, but they can only begin to help you when your leadership encourages the sharing of ideas and is willing to listen to them.

Sources

Buckley, Ronald L., *Winning in a Highly Competitive Manufacturing Environment*, Shady Brook Press, 2003

Deming, W. Edwards, *Out of the Crisis*, The MIT Press, 1982

Hallerstrom, Nils, *Modeling Aircraft Loans & Leases*, retrieved from: www.pkair.com, 2010

Porter, Michael, *The Five Competitive Forces that Shape Strategy*, Harvard Business Review, 1979

Welch, Jack, *Jack Straight from the Gut*, Warner Books, 2001

Womack, James P. and Jones, Daniel T., *Lean Manufacturing*, Simon and Schuster, 1996

www.ingramcontent.com/pod-product-compliance
Lightning Source LLC
Chambersburg PA
CBHW051503170526
45166CB00001B/361